£2.00

DANINA YOUNG

FROM TOM 1990.

D0513579

Edinburgh — Old Picture Postcards

EDINBURGH
FROM OLD PICTURE POSTCARDS

Andrew Cronshaw

MAINSTREAM
PUBLISHING

First published in Great Britain in 1989 by
MAINSTREAM PUBLISHING CO. (EDINBURGH) LTD.,
7 Albany Street
Edinburgh EH1 3UG

ISBN 1 85158 287 8 (cloth)

British Library Cataloguing in Publication Data
    Cronshaw, Andrew
    Edinburgh: old picture postcards
    1. Edinburgh, history
    I. Title
    941.3′4

    ISBN 1-85185-287-8

Design and layout by Paul Keir.
Reproduced from disc in typeface Goudy by Polyprint,
48 Pleasance, Edinburgh, EH8 9TJ.

Printed in Great Britain by Richard Clay Ltd.

To Family and Friends

ACKNOWLEDGEMENTS

The postcards were selected from the collections of Wilfred Grubb, Andrew Cronshaw, Ian White and Anthony Murray. The largest proportion of cards were taken from Wilfred Grubb's collection. Postcards which were used from the other collections are listed below:

(Key: T=Top, B=Bottom, C=Colour; e.g. 17T=Page 17, Top; C2=Card 2 in Colour Section)

Author's Collection
18, 19T; 20; 21T; 22; 23T; 25B; 27B; 29T; 30; 31T; 31B; 32; 35T; 35B; 40; 41B; 44T; 44B; 45B; 49T; 71T; 76; 90T; 92; 93T; 94; 98; 99T; 101B; 102; 103T; 104; 105T; 113B; 115T; 119B; 123T; C2; C3; C7.

Ian White's Collection
25T; 26; 41T; 45T; 54T; 54B; 59B; 68T; 82; 83B; 84T; 85B; 86T; 97T; 100; 103B; 109T; 112; 113T; C5; C6; C8.

Anthony Murray's Collection
17; 34; 57T; 99B.

Apologies for any inadvertent omission in attribution

FOREWORD

As one who has had a lifelong interest in pictorial record, having acquired my first camera at the age of eight and later, in my professional career, having promoted its cause through the medium of photographic competitions and otherwise, I was very pleased to be asked to contribute this foreword.

Andrew Cronshaw cut his teeth in this field, bookwise, in his *Old Dundee: Picture Postcards* in 1988 and found an ideal publisher in Mainstream. The result was an excellent production which I hope may be the first of many.

He continues the good work in exercising his talents on the Capital and I hope will follow it up still further! I could not fail to notice on visits to other Scottish towns, large and small, that the production of postcards of locai interest was by no means uncommon and hope for further coverage.

Meantime, the basis for such a series has had a most auspicious start.

C. S. MINTO
Formerly City Librarian and Curator
Edinburgh

INTRODUCTION

Edinburgh is a city to discover and to enjoy. This book attempts to explore and find out about the history of the city as it was in Victorian and Edwardian times and onwards to the early 1930s. Particular emphasis has been placed on scenes which have changed, buildings that have been demolished, villages which have become part of an expanding city, and the people who shaped Scotland's capital. Whilst some redevelopment of out-moded Victorian and Edwardian structures was to be expected many people regret that parts of the city have been irretrievably lost.

The City of Edinburgh and surrounding area has a long history of human habitation. The earliest farmers settled some time before 3000 BC. They introduced stock-rearing, agriculture and pottery making. Around 2000 BC the technique of using metal was introduced by settlers from the Continent. Shortly after 1000 BC, a period of conflict led to the construction of a number of hill forts. Such fortifications were built on Blackford Hill, Craiglockhart Hill, Corstorphine Hill and Castle Rock. The only known Roman fort in the area is at Cramond. It was constructed as an outpost of the Antonine Wall in 142 AD.

Castle Rock was the site of early settlements in the city. It was an ideal defensive location. The foundation of the burgh took place in the 12th century by expansion in an easterly direction. At every stage, growth was protected by the construction of defensive town walls.

By the end of the 15th century Edinburgh had become the Capital of Scotland. The population grew, leading to the development of suburbs. These were constructed south of Castle Rock in the Cowgate and Grassmarket. Expansion to the north was not possible because of the location of the Nor' Loch. However, the church community in the Canongate expanded up the hill from Holyrood. The last town wall to be built was the Flodden Wall. It was built after the defeat of the Scottish army in 1513. Its construction contained expansion of the city, leading to the building of tall tenements, overcrowding and poor health.

In 1603 the Scottish and English monarchies were united under James VI and I and the King resided south of the border. In 1707 the Scottish and English parliaments were unified. This proved unpopular with the Scots. It took until

1822 before William IV became the first monarch to visit Scotland since the union.

By the mid-18th century Edinburgh was recognised as being overcrowded, with a poor record of hygiene and health. A major development was required. Lord Provost George Drummond (1687-1766) proposed the building of an entirely New Town to the north of the Old Town. James Craig, a 22-year-old, virtually unknown architect, drew up a prize-winning design which was accepted in 1766. In 1767 construction of the New Town began. The Nor' Loch was partially drained and foundations were laid for the first North Bridge. The foundation stone for the bridge was laid by Lord Provost Drummond in 1763. Six years later an arch of the bridge collapsed. The bridge was rebuilt in 1872 and widened in 1873. It was demolished in 1895 and a second bridge constructed which opened in 1897.

Around 1830 the New Town, with its great squares, crescents, circuses, statues and promenades, was completed. Despite this expansion, Edinburgh, with a population of 138,000, was half the size of Glasgow.

The 19th and 20th centuries have seen expansion of the city in all directions, engulfing suburbs and remoter villages. In 1856 Edinburgh absorbed the small independent burghs of Canongate, Portsburgh and Calton. In 1896 Edinburgh absorbed Portobello, a coastal town east of the city. In 1920 Cramond, Gilmerton, Granton and Swanston were added and in 1975 Queensferry became part of the City of Edinburgh. Leith is the main port on the Firth of Forth and is situated to the north of Edinburgh. In 1329 it came under Edinburgh's control. It became an independent burgh in 1833 but became part of the City of Edinburgh in 1920. Between 1841 and 1911, the population of Edinburgh and Leith grew from 164,000 to 401,000 — much more than doubling. Glasgow's population increased three times over this period.

The 18th century and earlier years of the 19th century witnessed a coming together of great talents in the arts and sciences that later generations perspiciously dubbed the 'Enlightenment'. Artists, thinkers, architects and writers working in Edinburgh spread their influence far beyond the boundaries of Scotland. Great men of the period include the philosopher, David Hume (1711-1776); economist, Adam Smith (1723-1790); artist, Sir Henry Raeburn (1756-1823); author, Sir Walter Scott (1771-1832); engineer, James Nasmyth (1808-1890); surgeon, Joseph Lister (1827-1921) and physicist, James Clerk Maxwell (1831-1879).

Edinburgh also pioneered early developments of photography. William Henry Fox Talbot (1800-1877), working in England, developed the calotype process in 1841 but did not patent his invention in Scotland since there was a separate legal system and it would have proved too expensive to do so. This had interesting consequences which encouraged Edinburgh to become the centre of photography in world terms during the period that followed. In May 1842, John Adamson (1810-1870) succeeded in taking the first portrait calotype in Scotland using some of Talbot's ideas. John taught the new process to his brother, Robert Adamson (1821-1848) who set up a studio at Rock House, Calton Hill, in 1843. Painter David Octavius Hill (1802-1870), having been commissioned to produce a large canvas of members of the First General Assembly of the Free Protesting Church of Scotland, saw the advantages of using calotypes for producing likenesses instead of sketches. Hill went into partnership with Adamson.

By 1843 Hill and Adamson were totally competent in producing calotypes and they were of far higher quality than Talbot's pictures. Some of the earliest photographs taken by Hill and Adamson were of the building of the Scott Monument in 1844, Edinburgh architecture and Newhaven fisher-men and -women. The partnership survived until Adamson's death, at the age of 27, in 1848.

The Industrial Revolution of the 18th century saw an expansion in manufactured products. Increased output in the Victorian era led to several large Industrial Exhibitions throughout the country. In 1851 the first such exhibition was held at Crystal Palace in London. Edinburgh hosted two specialist exhibitions; on the subject of fisheries in 1882; and forestry in 1884. On 6 May 1886, H.R.H. Prince Albert Victor, Prince of Wales, opened the Meadows Exhibition. This International Exhibition of Industrial Science and Art occupied the whole of the West Meadows with seven acres of buildings and 18 acres of gardens and promenades. The exhibition closed in October of that year. It was well supported throughout the summer and gave a boost to local industries. In 1890 Edinburgh held an International Exhibition of Electrical Engineering, General Inventions and Industries at Meggetland, Colinton Road. In 1908, the Scottish National Exhibition, the last large exhibition, was held at Saughton.

Edinburgh is not a city which has evolved around heavy industry. The city's chief industry was printing, publishing and bookbinding. Examples include W. & R. Chambers Ltd., one of the oldest publishing houses in Britain, and cartographers John Bartholomew & Sons Ltd. Other traditional industries include brewing, rubber products such as golf balls, glass manufacture, paper and stationery, printing inks, food products and woollen textiles. Edinburgh is a centre of learning with a large number of private schools and a wide choice of higher education.

Edinburgh is a major tourist centre, which was as popular in Edwardian times as it is today. This is reflected by the number of postcards sent. The first British postcard was issued by the Post Office on 1 October 1870. Its monopoly hindered picture postcard development until 1894 when privately printed postcards for use with adhesive stamps were permitted. The first British view cards were produced in September 1894 by George Stewart & Co., Edinburgh. George Stewart was born in Dundee in 1834 where he had worked as a stationer. He later became a partner in the firm of George Waterson, Sons and Stewart of 56 and 60 Hanover Street. He founded his own firm, George Stewart & Co., at 92 George Street, on 1 October 1879. In 1886 he took advantage of the Edinburgh International Exhibition and won gold medals for his products. After George died in 1901, the business was run by his two sons, George Dalrymple Stewart and Alex Stewart, and John Muir, the Retail Manager. In 1912 Alex emigrated to New Zealand and in 1915 John Muir died. In 1926 George D. Stewart's son became Director of the firm.

The second Edinburgh firm to start publishing postcards in Edinburgh is likely to have been W. and A. K. Johnston Ltd., at their Edina Works, Easter Road. William and Alexander Keith Johnston founded a printing and engraving business in 1826. Alexander died in 1871. His brother, later Sir William Johnston, became Lord Provost of Edinburgh. They produced early court-sized postcards and many series during the Edwardian era.

Another Edinburgh postcard publisher is believed to have been J. A. M'Culloch and Co., Hillside Printing Works, Delhaig, Gorgie. It is thought that they were one firm that used the trademark 'Caledonia Series', but this series' title was also used by photographer and postcard publisher Marshal Wane, 82 George Street, Edinburgh. Marshal Wane had previously been the official photographer to the Meadows International Exhibition in 1886.

Edinburgh's most prolific postcard publisher was William Ritchie & Sons Ltd. William Ritchie was born at Cupar, Fife, in 1824. He was educated in Edinburgh and at the age of 19 he opened a bookshop in St Andrew Square. He later became a wholesale stationer at 16 Elder Street. He died at Strathspey on 3 September 1900. The business was continued by his two sons. They probably produced their first postcards around this time but production did not increase in scale until 1903. Cards produced at this time were lithographically printed with the 'Reliable Series' trademark. As techniques for postcard production were improved, real photograph postcards were introduced. William Ritchie & Sons were producing such cards around 1907, although some of the London publishing firms which specialised in this type of card were initially ahead of them in the technique. The original photographs used to show no clouds. The emulsions used at the time were slow and mainly sensitive to violet and blue light, so that the exposure time needed for the rest of the picture resulted in the sky being over-exposed. After development the sky came out unnaturally clear. This is shown in the photographic cards, but the clouds could be retouched by artists when the picture was to be lithographically printed.

Postcards with the 'Vello' trademark were produced by P. and W. Macniven Ltd. Peter and William Macniven started out as Nisbet and Macniven, owners of a paper mill at Balerno in 1770. In 1788 the firm moved to 23 Blair Street and established a warehouse for selling their paper which was more convenient for their customers. By 1821 Nisbet had dropped out and the firm was run by Peter and William. William died around 1844. His wife remarried very soon afterwards which led to a family dispute. Peter's son, John, was upset by this which resulted in the company splitting. John went into partnership as Macniven & Cameron Ltd. and took over the premises at 23 Blair Street. In the 1860s they established the 'Waverley' trademark for their pens and stationery. Their Waverley Works later occupied 23-33 Blair Street. William's widow remarried Mr Murray, who became manager of P. and W. Macniven Ltd. and they moved into 19 Blair Street. The firm produced postcards with the 'Vello' trademark until the firm ceased trading in 1909. They possibly produced the 'Waverley Series' postcards. Early cards were lithographically printed but later cards were real photographs. Macniven & Cameron Ltd. have no records of ever producing postcards. The 'Albany Series' of postcards gives no clue to its origin. Another Edinburgh publisher was J. R. Russell, a wholesale stationer based at 25 North Bridge Street. He first issued postcards in 1903 and continued throughout the Edwardian period. William Nimmo & Co., 46 Constitution Street, Leith, published several series of Edinburgh postcards, using photographs taken by local photographers Alex A. Inglis and James Patrick. The earliest real photographic postcards appear to have been produced by the national chain of photographers, A. & G. Taylor, in 1904. It is important to note, by the way, that the dates given in this book refer to the date when the photograph was taken and not when the card was issued. Certain pictures would be used for several years and then updated. Others, where the view had not changed, would be kept in production for several decades.

Until 1897 no message was allowed on the address side; the picture on the front was reduced in size to leave space for the message. In 1902 the 'divided' back card was introduced in Britain, allowing the message and address to be written on the same side. The heyday of the picture postcard in Britain, which developed into a collecting craze, was between 1895 and 1915. By 1903 some 600 million cards were sent annually. This peaked at 880 million in 1914. On 3 June 1918 the price of sending a postcard doubled to 1d. In the year that followed half the previous year's number of postcards were sent. The cards, mostly costing 1d each, occupied the role of the telephone today. Local deliveries were frequent. It was common to have at least four collections a day with guaranteed same-day delivery within a local area. As pictures and photographs were rare in newspapers, postcards provided an attraction to the sender, especially if their street, house or they themselves appeared on the card. One of the fascinations of old postcards today is the quiet, peaceful way of life they record. Even in a busy capital city like Edinburgh there appears to be no sense of urgency or rush.

Old postcards provide a further interest through their messages which reflect aspects of the period in which they were sent. Writing to her sister in Berwickshire in 1904, a young girl says: 'I was at Princes Street and did some shopping this morning. After dinner M and D walked down to Blair's and got back for tea. It has been very windy today especially in Princes Street.' Visitors in Edinburgh in August 1924 sent a card home with the message: 'This card shows the hansom cab in which Grannie and Eve drove back to 41 Drumsheugh Gardens. Grannie said she drove in one of the first hansoms and she drove in this which must be one of the last.'

Princes Street has changed drastically since the turn of the century. Architecturally fine buildings have been destroyed and most of the traditional Edinburgh proprietors have been replaced by modern chain store equivalents. Characteristic shops on Princes Street once included Andrew Elliot's bookshop; the tobacconists, David Simpson and John Sinclair; R. W. Forsyth's departmental store; Rentons the drapers; John Ford & Co., glass and china merchants; Milne's Ltd., the stationers; Mackay and Chisholm, gold and silversmiths; G. Ballantyne & Co., tea dealers and wine merchants; J. W. Mackie & Sons, bakers; John Wight, costumiers; and James Ritchie & Son, watch and clock makers. Princes Street at one time boasted four picture houses. Many shoppers and picture-goers met at Maules. The story of Robert Maule & Son Ltd. is symptomatic of many successful businesses. In 1856 Sir Robert Maule's father opened a retail shop in Kincardine-on-Forth. In 1872 he moved to Leith, taking his son into partnership. In 1878 and in 1892 they extended their business premises which resulted in a move to 146 Princes Street. Sir Robert Maule died in December 1931 and the store was left in the hands of trustees until it was taken over by H. Binns & Son & Co. Ltd. of Sunderland on 5 May 1937. The House of Fraser subsequently took over Binns in April 1953.

Selecting postcards for this book has taken a considerable amount of time. Vast numbers of postcards of Edinburgh were published at the turn of the century and it appears that many still survive in old albums and collections. The vast majority of these cards however are of Princes Street, the Castle and the Royal Mile. Whilst including some of the best of these cards in this book it has been the intention to show rarer pictures which explore Edinburgh's residential areas and some of the outlying villages and suburbs which now form part of today's capital.

I would like to thank the following people for their invaluable assistance and support which enabled me to prepare this book: Wilfred Grubb, Ian White, and Anthony Murray for the loan of postcards from their collections; Sara Stevenson and Julie Lawson, Scottish Photography Archive, Scottish National Portrait Gallery, Edinburgh; and the Edinburgh Room librarians, Central Library, George IV Bridge.

For their apt comments and suggestions I thank J. F. Birrell; Malcolm Cant; Waverley Cameron; Ray Footman; Frank Gerstenberg; C. W. Hill; D. L. G. Hunter; Elizabeth and Linda Kerr; Forbes Macgregor; Charles McKean; C. S. Minto; A. Reid; Charles J. Smith; T. C. Smout; David Walker; and Bruce Young. Thanks are extended to Fiona Curle for typing the text.

Andrew Cronshaw
Edinburgh
June 1989

'SIGNPOST' CARD *circa 1910*

This postcard was produced by Birn Brothers, London. Joseph and Sigmund Birn started business as stationers in London in 1882. They produced their first postcards around 1903, many of which were printed in Germany. London was the main publishing centre in Great Britain for postcards during the Edwardian era. Most of the publishing houses were situated in the 'Postcard Mile', an area of about one square mile, just north of St Paul's Cathedral. A consequence of this location was that many firms that survived until the Second World War were devastated during enemy air raids. Many photographic plates, artwork and records were destroyed as a result. However, Edinburgh is believed to have had the second largest number of postcard publishers after London. Although Edinburgh postcard publishers were many in number no single firm could match the vast output of James Valentine and Sons of Dundee.

Edinburgh Castle and Esplanade.   RELIABLE 🛡 SERIES. 137(

ABOVE: *EDINBURGH CASTLE AND ESPLANADE circa 1904*
Castle Rock was fortified before the Roman invasion. Since that time Romans, Saxons, Picts, Celts, English and Scots have claimed it as the reward of victory. The Castle gateway, with moat and drawbridge, is seen in front. Above this is the Half Moon Battery, where the Time Gun is fired, Queen Mary's apartments are on the left and the State Prison is on the extreme left. The Esplanade was constructed as a parade ground in the early 19th century. It was a place of execution in earlier times.

TOP RIGHT: *FIRING THE TIME GUN, EDINBURGH CASTLE circa 1905*
The firing of the One O'Clock Gun from the battlements of the Castle started on 7 June 1861. Simultaneously, one can also see the falling of the time-ball on the mast of the Nelson Monument, on Calton Hill. Originally each of these time devices was controlled by electrical impulses sent from the Royal Observatory on Calton Hill. Nowadays the time-ball is released manually when the gun is fired in response to a signal from Greenwich.

BOTTOM RIGHT: *LAWNMARKET circa 1905*
The spire in the background belongs to the Tolbooth Church and is the highest spire in Edinburgh. Among the most interesting of the Lawnmarket's historic alleys are Riddle's, Brodie's and Baxter's Closes and James's Court. Deacon William Brodie (1741-1788), born in Brodie's Close, was a respectable Town Councillor by day and dangerous criminal by night. He is likely to have been the inspiration for R. L. Stevenson's *Dr Jekyll and Mr Hyde*. Robert Burns (1759-1796) lodged in Baxter's Close on his first visit to Edinburgh.

HALF-MOON BATTERY, EDINBURGH CASTLE, FIRING THE TIME GUN. 1173

The Lawnmarket, Edinburgh.

ABOVE: ST GILES CATHEDRAL *circa 1878*
The 'Hie Kirk' of St Giles occupies the north side of Parliament Square. The present building rose on the foundations of an earlier Norman church burned by the English in 1385. John Knox was amongst its post-reformation pastors. In 1637 Jenny Geddes threw her stool at Dean Hanna who attempted to conduct an Episcopal service. During the temporary period of Episcopacy it became a Cathedral. A donation from Sir William Chambers, the publisher, enabled restoration work to be carried out at the beginning of this century.

TOP RIGHT: EDINBURGH TOLBOOTH (*The Heart of Midlothian*) *circa 1810*
Edinburgh Tolbooth, situated to the west of St Giles Cathedral, was demolished in 1817. Today its site is indicated by brass plates in the road and a heart-shaped design of sets. The oldest part of the Tolbooth may have dated from the late 14th century. During its existence it was the meeting place of the Scottish Parliament and Edinburgh Town Council. It was also used as a courthouse, gaol and place of execution.

BOTTOM RIGHT: MERCAT CROSS AND CITY CHAMBERS *circa 1915*
The Mercat Cross was re-erected on its octagonal base in 1885 by William Gladstone (1809-1898). It was the scene of executions and a place from which Royal proclamations were, and still are, made. Behind stand the City Chambers. They were designed by John Adam and completed in 1761. Today the building is occupied by the City of Edinburgh District Council. Beneath the building, in its cellars, Mary King's Close can still be seen.

THE OLD TOLBOOTH (THE HEART OF MIDLOTHIAN) KNOX SERIES

Mercat Cross & City Chambers, Edinburgh. Knox Series.

ABOVE: LOWER HIGH STREET circa 1910
This view of the High Street is taken looking in the direction of the Castle from a spot near John Knox's House. A company of the Black Watch is seen marching down towards Holyrood. The Tron Church, in the middle distance, was built in 1637. The spire was restored, after destruction by fire in 1824. The Tron was named after the 'trone' or weighing machine for salt which stood outside the church.

TOP RIGHT: JOHN KNOX'S HOUSE circa 1878
John Knox (1505-1572) was ordained minister of St Giles in 1560. He stayed at different times in the Old Fleshmarket and Warriston Closes and later, it is claimed, in his residence shown here near the Netherbow. The timber-fronted building is a fine example of domestic architecture of the 16th century. The Reformer was buried in St Giles Churchyard, now Parliament Close.

BOTTOM RIGHT: HUNTLY HOUSE, CANONGATE circa 1910
The Huntly family resided in part of this building in the mid-18th century. The present street frontage was established in 1570 when three separate adjacent houses were joined to form one property. The building was restored by the city in 1932 and became the principal local history museum.

ABOVE: CANONGATE circa 1912
Moray House, on the right beyond the washing poles, was built in the early 17th century. In 1645 the house was inherited by Margaret, Countess of Moray. Today it forms part of the College of Education. The building on the left with the clock is the Canongate Tolbooth built in 1591. This photograph was taken and printed by Judges' Ltd., Hastings, but was published by William Ritchie and Sons Ltd., Edinburgh.

TOP RIGHT: ABBEY STRAND circa 1903
The two adjoining 17th-century buildings on the left are the last survivors of a group of buildings which once clustered around the Palace. There is a triple 's' in the road at the head of Abbey Strand. It was in these houses that debtors and others faced with prosecution under civil law obtained sanctuary. This stopped in 1880 when imprisonment for debt ceased. The Palace yard gates were built in 1922 as a memorial to King Edward VII.

BOTTOM RIGHT: HOLYROOD PALACE circa 1907
Holyrood Abbey, now in ruins, was founded by David I of Scots in 1128. It was repeatedly burnt and plundered by English armies and in civil wars and was the scene of many historic events. The Palace of Holyrood House was built by James IV in 1502 and was subsequently extended by James V around 1525. Mary Queen of Scots lived at Holyrood from 1564-70.

The Abbey Strand. Holyrood. EDINBURGH.

84.

HOLYROOD PALACE AND ARTHUR SEAT. EDINBURGH. RELIABLE SERIES 340 / 54

ABOVE: GREYFRIARS BOBBY circa 1915

Bobby was a Skye terrier owned by John Gray, a police constable, who lived at Hall's Court in the Cowgate. Gray acquired Bobby as a puppy around 1856. One of John Gray's duties was to guard livestock brought into the Grassmarket for the weekly Wednesday market. Each of the four policemen involved in this job owned a dog. In the autumn of 1857, John Gray became ill. He was attended to by Police Surgeon Dr Henry Littlejohn, who later became Edinburgh's first Medical Officer of Health. However, John Gray died of tuberculosis on 8 February 1858 and was buried in Greyfriars Churchyard. Bobby was present at the funeral on 10 February 1858. After being taken back to the Grays' home he escaped and returned to his master's grave. The next day Bobby was found back in the churchyard. This was the start of a 14-year vigil. Bobby was fed by a succession of owners of a restaurant at 6 Greyfriars Place. Bobby died in the house of restaurant-owner John Traill in 1872 and was buried in Greyfriars Churchyard. The memorial fountain was unveiled on 15 November 1873 but the water supply was discontinued in 1957.

CASTLE FROM GREYFRIARS CHURCHYARD *circa 1915*

FOOT OF WEST BOW, GRASSMARKET *circa 1915*

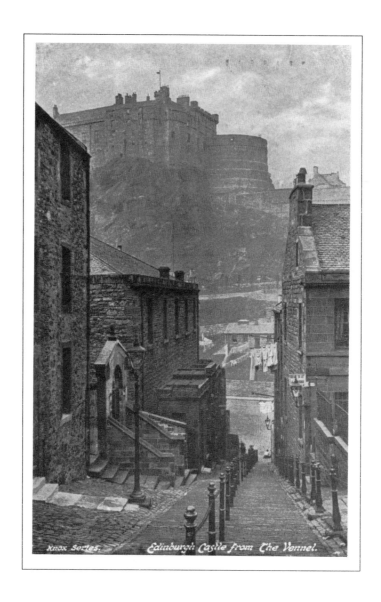

ABOVE: CASTLE FROM THE VENNEL circa 1915

TOP RIGHT: CASTLE FROM GRASSMARKET circa 1878
The Grassmarket was in earlier times the market place of Edinburgh. It was the scene of many public executions. In its inns Wordsworth and other guests found accommodation. Robert Burns stayed here for eight days in November 1791 on his last visit to Edinburgh. The picture shows the 'Black Bull lodgings for travellers and working men', the 'Beehive Hotel' and the 'Clydesdale Inn'.

BOTTOM RIGHT: GRASSMARKET AND CASTLE circa 1904
The Flodden Wall skirted the western end of the Grassmarket and the West Port opened off it. In Tanners Close, off the Grassmarket, William Burke and William Hare prepared the corpses which they sold to surgeons for medical research. Hare later confessed to the crimes and saved his life. Burke was hanged in the Grassmarket on 28 January 1829 before a crowd of 20,000.

THE GRASSMARKET & CASTLE

Calton Hill.   Edinburgh.

Thence we had a very fine view.

Printed in Saxony 1864

ABOVE: *CALTON HILL circa 1880*
The monument to Lord Nelson crowns Calton Hill. Other monuments on Calton Hill include the uncompleted National Monument, Professor Dugald Stewart's monument and Calton Observatory. On the left is Rock House Studio where artist David Octavius Hill and photographer Robert Adamson worked. The studio was subsequently occupied in the 1870s by Archibald Burns and later by Alex Inglis, some of whose photographs appeared as postcards.

TOP RIGHT: *VIEW FROM CALTON HILL circa 1878*
The building on the left is Calton Prison and beyond this is Old Calton burial ground. The Obelisk was erected to 'Political Martyrs' of 1793. Princes Street on the right appears to end, in this picture, with St Mary's Cathedral. Other sights include the crown of St Giles, the Tolbooth Church steeple and the Castle. The North British Station Hotel, built in 1902, now obscures the view of the Scott Monument.

BOTTOM RIGHT: *REGISTER HOUSE AND WATERLOO PLACE circa 1908*
The building of Register House was begun in 1774 from the designs of Robert Adam. It occupied the site of the old village of Moultrie's Hill. With the adjacent Register House behind, it accommodates the national records of Scotland. In front is an equestrian statue of the Duke of Wellington, designed by Sir John Steell. The unveiling took place on 18 June 1852, the anniversary of Waterloo.

H.M. REGISTER HOUSE.
EDINBURGH.

ABOVE: WAVERLEY MARKET FROM SCOTT MONUMENT *circa 1878*
Waverley Market opened in 1868. It was initially an open market selling fruit and vegetables.
It was covered and the roof laid out as an ornamental garden in June 1877. The garden was
planted out with more than 7,000 flowering shrubs, complete with wrought iron benches and
drinking fountains. The picture shows the buildings beyond the market which were demolished
to make way for the North British Station Hotel, which opened on 16 October 1902.

TOP RIGHT: PRINCES STREET SHOWING SCOTT MONUMENT *circa 1904*
Sir Walter Scott was recognised during his lifetime as the greatest figure in Scottish literature.
Born in Edinburgh in 1771, he became a barrister and was made Sheriff of Selkirkshire. He
published his first novel, *Waverley*, anonymously in 1814 and kept his authorship of succeeding
novels secret for several years. He died at Abbotsford on 21 September 1832 and was buried at
Dryburgh Abbey. The Scott Monument in Princes Street Gardens was erected in 1840-44 at a
cost of £16,000.

BOTTOM RIGHT: PRINCES STREET *circa 1907*
The picture shows cable car 137 travelling towards the photographer. The cable-car system
involved running an endless cable in a sunken conduit at road level between the tram lines.
The cable travelled around the city at about eight mph, powered by winding drums situated at
Henderson Row, and later from Shrubhill. Each tram lowered a 'gripper' on to the cable when
the driver wished to move forward and this was released when the tram wished to stop. The
system was cheap to run and avoided overhead wires in Princes Street.

Princes Street, looking East, Edinburgh.

THE OLD RAILWAY STATION

ABOVE: OLD RAILWAY STATION circa 1860
Waverley Market was constructed on the site of Canal Street Station, which had been built by the Edinburgh, Leith and Newhaven Railway Company. The line was extended to Canal Street from Scotland Street by the construction of a tunnel under Drummond Place, Dublin Street and St Andrew Square. Opening in 1846, north-bound carriages were controlled by a break wagon and south-bound trains were hauled uphill by a six-inch rope powered by a stationary steam engine. Canal Street Station and tunnel closed around 1865.

TOP RIGHT: CASTLE AND NATIONAL GALLERY FROM SCOTT MONUMENT 1890
A fine view of Castle Rock is obtained from the Scott Monument. The National Gallery on the Mound is shown below with the Royal Institution partly shown on the right. Each of these two buildings was designed by William Playfair, the former in 1845, the latter in 1822-26. In 1911 the Royal Scottish Academy took over the Royal Institution building.

BOTTOM RIGHT: FLORAL CLOCK, PRINCES STREET GARDENS circa 1905
In 1902 this site was laid out as a floral crown as a tribute to the Coronation of King Edward VII. From this display grew the idea of a floral clock. In 1903 a clock, with one hand, was installed by James Ritchie and Son of Edinburgh. The following year the clock had two hands and in 1905 a cuckoo mechanism was installed, but it was found that it could not be heard against the noise of traffic in Princes Street.

34

Princes Street from the West, Edinburgh. 643

ABOVE: PRINCES STREET, WEST END *circa 1925*

Princes Street shown here is beginning to look congested. Horse-drawn transport is on its way out with the appearance of motor cars, taxis and electric trams. The picture shows Edinburgh's first drinking fountain for men, horses and dogs, established by Catherine Sinclair, an energetic social worker, who is remembered by a monument in Queen Street. The fountain was removed as it became a danger to traffic and never re-sited.

TOP RIGHT: PRINCES STREET, WEST END *circa 1903*

The church in the centre of the picture is St John's Episcopal Church. To its right is 'St Cuthbert's under the Castle', generally known as the West Kirk. The oldest part of this church is its spire which dates from about 1789. The cable car in the centre is turning into Princes Street from Lothian Road. Rails were first laid in Princes Street for horse-drawn trams in November 1871. The first Edinburgh Street Tramway Company horse tram service ran from Haymarket to Bernard Street, Leith, on 6 November 1871.

BOTTOM RIGHT: CALEDONIAN HOTEL *circa 1924*

In 1845 Caledonian Railway trains terminated in a wooden structure on the site of today's Sheraton Hotel. On 2 May 1870 a temporary station was built at the west end of Princes Street. A new station was constructed in the 1880s. The Caledonian Hotel was subsequently built on top of this station and opened on 21 December 1903. The last train to depart from the Caledonian Station left for Birmingham on 4 September 1965.

Edinburgh from West.

CALEDONIAN HOTEL, EDINBURGH

GEORGE STREET, EDINBURGH.

SUTHERLAND'S
K.A. SERIES

ABOVE: GEORGE STREET LOOKING EAST TO ST ANDREW SQUARE circa 1925
This is one of the finest New Town streets, which runs along the summit of a ridge parallel to Princes Street. At its intersections, from which fine views can be obtained of the Firth of Forth, are placed statues of George IV, William Pitt, and Dr Chalmers. George IV's statue is shown here on the left. Beyond it is St Andrew Square. Tramcars were introduced to George Street in July 1925.

TOP RIGHT: GEORGE STREET LOOKING WEST TO CHARLOTTE SQUARE circa 1903
St Andrew's Church, shown on the right, was designed by Major Andrew Fraser after winning a design competition in 1785. It was the scene of the Disruption of the Church of Scotland General Assembly in 1843. The Edinburgh Institution was founded in George Street in 1832. In 1920 it moved to Melville Street where it became Melville College. In 1972 it joined with Daniel Stewart's to become Stewart's Melville College.

BOTTOM RIGHT: LADIES COLLEGE, QUEEN STREET circa 1903
The first Merchant Company school, the Merchant Maiden Hospital, was founded in the Cowgate by Mary Erskine in 1694. In 1818 the school moved to Archibald Place. In 1871 George Watson's Hospital took over this site and the school moved to 70-72 Queen Street. The name Edinburgh Ladies College was adopted in 1889, which later changed to Queen Street School, and then to Mary Erskine School for Girls in 1944. The school moved to the grounds of Ravelston House in 1966. In the distance stands the Gothic Monument to Catherine Sinclair (1800-1864).

George Street, Edinburgh.

Ladies' College, Queen Street.

Edinburgh.

J. M. Edinburgh.

St. Mary's Cathedral,
Edinburgh

ABOVE: ST MARY'S CATHEDRAL 1894

St Mary's Episcopal Cathedral was designed by Sir George Gilbert Scott (1811-1878) and completed by his son. Funds for the construction were bequeathed by Barbara and Mary Walker of Easter Coates. The Cathedral was consecrated on 29 October 1879. The two smaller spires were finally completed during the First World War. The old Jacobean Manor House of Easter Coates, which stands nearby in Cathedral Close, now houses St Mary's Music School.

TOP RIGHT: MANOR PLACE, circa 1905

BOTTOM RIGHT: DEAN BRIDGE circa 1904

Dean village was originally named Village of the Water of Leith. It was once the largest of Edinburgh's flour-milling settlements. Its earliest mills date back to the 16th century. Its decline began in the late 19th century as the larger, modern flour mills developed in Leith. Today many of the old mills have been turned into flats conserving the character of the area. The picture shows Dean Bridge, which was built by Thomas Telford in 1832.

Manor Place, Edinburgh

DEAN BRIDGE, EDINBURGH.

Edinburgh, Entrance Waverley Station

ABOVE: WAVERLEY STATION circa 1904
The Edinburgh and Glasgow Railway Company opened a line to Haymarket in 1842. Tunnels at Haymarket and at the Mound were completed in 1846 enabling trains to run along the valley of the Nor' Loch. Waverley Station was opened by the North British Railway Company, the new owners of the line, in March 1848. The station was rebuilt in 1893.

TOP RIGHT: NEW NORTH BRIDGE AND SCOTSMAN BUILDINGS circa 1905
The original North Bridge was opened in 1772 and was the first direct link between the Old and New Towns. The new, wider and improved bridge was completed in 1897. Fronting the southern part of the bridge are the Carlton Hotel on the left and *The Scotsman* buildings on the right. *The Scotsman* was first published, from the High Street, in 1817. Publication from its present site began in 1904.

BOTTOM RIGHT: SCOTSMAN DELIVERY TRICYCLES 1912
In 1912 high-speed delivery of evening newspapers was by Phanomobil — front-wheel drive tricycles. A variable friction drive off the engine's flywheel enabled the 8,800 c.c. 'v' twin engine to power its load at moderate speed and to tackle Edinburgh's hills without a gearbox. A fleet of Model T Fords later replaced the tricycles. The headlines on the boards of the delivery bikes read: 'Scenes at Marconi inquiry, Premier's letter, conspiracy charge against suffragettes'.

NORTH BRIDGE, EDINBURGH.

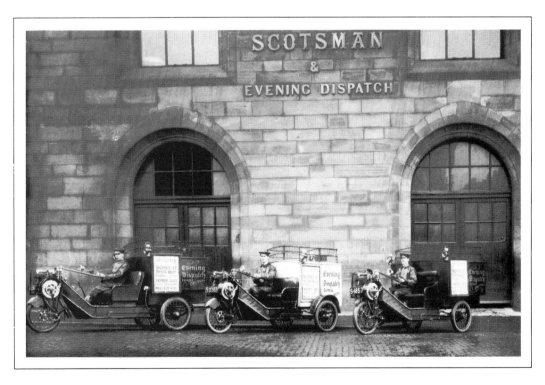

HOPE PARK TERRACE *circa 1903*
SOUTH CLERK STREET *circa 1903*

MAYFIELD ROAD *circa* 1903

MAYFIELD ROAD *circa* 1903

45

St Leonard's Entrance. Kings Park. Edinburgh.

ABOVE: ARTHUR'S SEAT 1905

Arthur's Seat, the lion-shaped hill, may have derived its name from King Arthur. Consisting of hard, resistant igneous rock, it is one of the many extinct volcanoes in Central Scotland. Two centres of eruption may be recognised, the older being the Lion's Head vent, and the younger and more extensive, the Lion's Haunch. Salisbury Crags, to the left, form an independent intrusion. The granite drinking fountain, gifted by Mrs Nichol of Huntly Lodge, Morningside, dates from April 1886.

TOP RIGHT: LEMONADE VENDOR circa 1905

A familiar sight in Edwardian times was the lemonade vendor at the top of Arthur's Seat. In March 1862 plans were made to construct a tea-house or restaurant beside Queen's Drive near Dunsapie Loch. At the time the idea caused an outcry and the plan was abandoned.

BOTTOM RIGHT: WELLS O' WEARIE, HOLYROOD PARK circa 1908

The railway line in the foreground is part of the 'Innocent Railway' which opened in July 1831. It was originally constructed by engineer James Jardine (1776-1858) to carry coal and agricultural products from Newtongrange, Dalkeith and Musselburgh to St Leonard's Depot, Edinburgh. Passengers were carried to Dalkeith for 6d from 1832-1845. During this period no passengers were killed, giving the railway the title of 'Innocent'. The line closed in August 1968.

At the top of Arthur's Seat, King's Park, Edinburgh

Wells o' Wearie, King's Park, Edinburgh.

DUDDINGSTON.

ABOVE: DUDDINGSTON *crica 1907*

Duddingston was once a busy weaving centre where a coarse linen cloth known as 'Duddingston hardings' was produced. Prince Charlie held a council of war in one of the houses in the village in September 1745 before the Battle of Prestonpans. The 'Sheep's Heid Inn' is believed to have been one of the oldest inns in Scotland. An inn has stood on the site since the 16th century. The present building is mainly 19th century.

TOP RIGHT: DUDDINGSTON CHURCH *circa 1904*

Duddingston Church was built in 1143. It was once the home of landscape painter Rev. John Thomson, minister from 1805 to 1840. Visitors have included J. M. W. Turner and Sir Walter Scott, an elder of the Kirk, who wrote part of *The Heart of Midlothian* in the Manse garden. The church overlooks Duddingston Loch which was used for curling in the winter and since 1923 has been a bird sanctuary.

BOTTOM RIGHT: STATION ROAD, CRAIGMILLAR *circa 1904*

The picture shows Craigmillar Station which formed part of the inner suburban railway. The inner line ran from Waverley to Haymarket, passed through Gorgie, Craiglockhart, Morningside Road, Blackford Hill, Newington, Duddingston, Craigmillar and then by main line via Portobello, Piershill, Abbeyhill and back to Waverley. Craigmillar Station was originally built for members of Edinburgh Insurance and Banking Golf Club whose course was nearby.

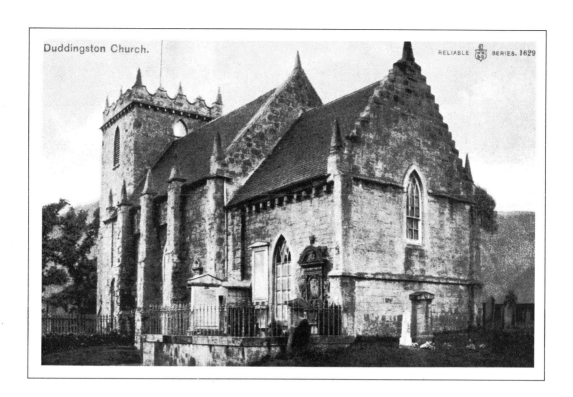

Duddingston Church.

RELIABLE SERIES. 1629

STATION ROAD, CRAIGMILLAR.

CRAIGMILLAR CASTLE, EDINBURGH.

ABOVE: CRAIGMILLAR CASTLE circa 1913
Mary Queen of Scots (1542-1587) stayed at Craigmillar Castle in September 1563 and again in late 1566. It was here that the plot was made to murder the Queen's husband, Lord Darnley. During Mary's reign the castle was owned by Sir Simon Preston, Lord Provost of Edinburgh from 1565-69. In 1660 the barony of Craigmillar was bought by Sir John Gilmour. In 1946 his descendant, Sir John Little Gilmour, handed the castle over to the Scottish Office.

TOP RIGHT: LITTLE FRANCE AND QUEEN MARY'S TREE, CRAIGMILLAR circa 1903
This old sycamore tree, at Little France on the Old Dalkeith Road, was known as 'Queen Mary's tree'. Mary Queen of Scots may have planted it or rested under it when she visited or stayed at Craigmillar. Today the tree has gone, but the cottage, with the two chimneys, still remains. Craigmillar Castle is situated just off the right of the picture, on the brow of the hill.

BOTTOM RIGHT: CROSSROADS, GILMERTON circa 1907
Records of the settlement of Gilmerton date back to the 16th century. Its development, until recent times, has been associated with coal-mining and quarrying of limestone. Dr Guthrie, founder of the concept of Ragged Schools, is remembered in Gilmerton, with the establishment of Dr Guthrie's Girls' Industrial School in 1904. In 1847, Dr Thomas Guthrie (1803-1873) acquired rooms in Ramsay Lane, Castlehill, where he was able to feed, clothe and educate needy young boys and girls.

CROSS ROADS. GILMERTON.

LIBERTON FROM THE AIR

ABOVE: LIBERTON FROM THE AIR circa 1918
Beyond the village of Liberton can just be seen the Royal Observatory on Blackford Hill which opened in 1896. To the right of this, the site of Edinburgh University's King's Buildings is seen as just a field. The University purchased the site two miles south of Old College in 1919 to accommodate the rapid growth of science teaching and research. King George V laid the foundation stone for the first building, the Chemistry Department, in 1920. King's Buildings took their name after this event.

TOP RIGHT: LIBERTON circa 1913
Liberton is possibly named after an old leper hospital once located in the area. In the distance stands Liberton Kirk, built around 1815. On 20 June 1922 an electric tram route started from Pilrig to Nether Liberton. This new electrification was initially unpopular. As this tram entered Nicolson Street it was forced to a halt by students who had formed a blockage across the rails. The tram was then bombarded with bags of flour. The tram eventually reached Nether Liberton but the protest had not been anticipated by the organisers.

BOTTOM RIGHT: LIBERTON BRAE circa 1913
The steepness of the hill is indicated by the cyclist pushing his bicycle uphill and the special tracks, on the right, which were laid to enable horses and carts to get a better grip of the road surface. The nearest destination for cable-cars at this time was Nether Liberton on level ground. However, in 1924 electric tramcars ran to the top of Liberton Brae. On 1 June 1929 a tramcar lost control going downhill and crashed into 40 Liberton Brae.

LIBERTON

LIBERTON BRAE.

MARCHMONT ROAD, EDINBURGH.

340 / 476

Marchmont Road from Meadows, Edinburgh. 77539 JV

MARCHMONT ROAD *circa 1907*

MARCHMONT ROAD FROM MEADOWS *1913*

WARRENDER PARK ROAD AND USHER INSTITUTE circa 1907

STRATHEARN ROAD circa 1904

FIRST CABLE CAR ENTERING POLWARTH GARDENS 7 April 1908

SHANDON TERRACE, NORTH MERCHISTON circa 1914

TOLLCROSS *circa 1904*

ASHLEY TERRACE, NORTH MERCHISTON *circa 1914*

Merchiston Castle, Edinburgh.

ABOVE: *MERCHISTON CASTLE, COLINTON ROAD circa 1904*
Merchiston Castle was acquired by Alexander Napier in 1438. John Napier (1550-1617), the inventor of logarithms, was born in the castle. In 1833 Merchiston Castle School leased the castle and grounds. The school was founded by Charles Chalmers, a successful publisher, who was forced to retire from publishing due to ill health. On 1 October 1930 the school transferred to Colinton House estate. In 1964 the castle was restored and became part of Napier Polytechnic.

TOP RIGHT: *MORNINGSIDE ROAD AND CHRISTCHURCH circa 1904*
The nearby Bruntsfield Hospital was founded in 1885 by Scotland's first woman doctor, Sophia Jex-Blake (1840-1912) as the Free Hospital for Women and Children. In 1869 Sophia and five other girls were reluctantly admitted to study medicine at Edinburgh University. In 1872 the University refused to allow the women to sit their exams. Sophia was forced to depart for Switzerland where she graduated from Berne University in 1877. In March 1878 she returned to Edinburgh and opened a practice at 4 Manor Place.

BOTTOM RIGHT: *MORNINGSIDE circa 1903*
The picture shows Morningside Station on the left. Thomas Bouch (1822-1880) was responsible for the plan of the Suburban Railway which opened on 1 December 1884. The railway was first promoted as a separate company and known as Edinburgh Suburban and Southside Junction Railway. It was subsequently absorbed by the North British Railway Company. The inner and outer circle lines closed to passengers on 10 September 1962.

58

ABOVE: BRAIDBURN DAIRY, BRAID ROAD circa 1904
The picture shows Braidburn dairy on the site now occupied by Mortonhall Tennis Club. In 1904 there were over 400 dairy keepers in the Edinburgh area. Each dairy would have a few cows and serve only one or two streets with milk. Town dairies disappeared as stricter health regulations were introduced. The campaign against tuberculosis started in the 1930s. More efficient farming and improved transportation and storage also helped to reduce the number of dairies.

TOP RIGHT: BUCKSTONE FARM AND MORNINGSIDE circa 1904
The picture shows the Comiston Road-Braid Road fork as a quiet rural scene. Over the brow of Braid Road one can approach Braid Hills golf courses. As Edinburgh expanded southwards in the late 19th century, development began to occur around Bruntsfield Links which led to restrictions on golfers. In 1888 the Town Council purchased a portion of the Braid Hills from the Braid Hills estate. The golf course was formally opened on 29 May 1889. Tommy Armour, born in Edinburgh in 1896, was one of many famous players to use the course. At the age of 14 he was one of the best boy golfers in Britain. He became British Open Champion in 1931.

BOTTOM RIGHT: LANARK ROAD, JUNIPER GREEN circa 1924
Juniper Green may have been named after the many juniper bushes in the area of the village. In the 16th century flax, grain, paper and snuff mills operated along the valley of the Water of Leith. On 1 August 1874 Juniper Green Station was opened by the Caledonian Railway Company. Improved communications with Edinburgh saw the development of large detached houses on both sides of Lanark Road.

Buckstone Farm & Morningside.

LANARK ROAD. JUNIPER GREEN

SWANSTON COTTAGE,
AN EARLY HOME OF R.L. STEVENSON.

ABOVE: SWANSTON COTTAGE circa 1907

Robert Louis Stevenson (1850-1894) was born at 8 Howard Place, Edinburgh, as the son of Thomas Stevenson, a civil engineer, and Margaret Balfour, a minister's daughter. In 1857 the Stevensons moved to 17 Heriot Row, Edinburgh, where the family stayed until Thomas's death in 1887. The family leased Swanston Cottage in the spring of 1857. For the next 14 years they used it as a holiday home.

TOP RIGHT: SWANSTON circa 1907

In the autumn of 1867 R. L. Stevenson became an undergraduate in engineering at Edinburgh University. In 1870 he changed to study law and announced his intention to become a professional writer. Showing little interest in becoming an Edinburgh advocate, he travelled widely in Scotland, Europe and America, usually in pursuit of better health. Stevenson's most celebrated books include: *Treasure Island, Kidnapped, A Child's Garden of Verses* and *Dr Jekyll and Mr Hyde*.

BOTTOM RIGHT: SWANSTON circa 1907

Swanston today still preserves its rural atmosphere with a group of thatched 17th-century cottages, farmhouse and school. James Patrick took this photograph which is one of a series of studies he made of Swanston. He was the son of Fife photographer, John Patrick (1830-1923). In 1895 James Patrick established a photographic studio at 40 Braid Road. From 1896 to 1907 his studio was in Comiston Road.

A SHEPHERDS CARE.   JAMES PATRICK.

"SWEET IS THE BREATH OF THE NEW MOWN HAY"   JAMES PATRICK.

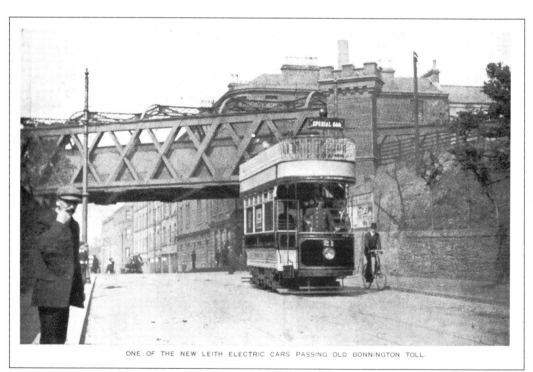

ONE OF THE NEW LEITH ELECTRIC CARS PASSING OLD BONNINGTON TOLL.

EDINBURGH CABLE CAR, GORGIE ROAD circa 1910

LEITH ELECTRIC TRAMCAR, OLD BONNINGTON TOLL, August 1905

ABOVE: ROYAL REVIEW 18 September 1905
The Royal Review of Scottish Volunteers by King Edward VII was one of the greatest military spectacles of the century. Nearly 40,000 volunteers from all over Scotland passed in review before the Sovereign in Holyrood Park. Hundreds of thousands of spectators watched the events from the natural amphitheatre of Arthur's Seat. The King arrived on horseback dressed in Field Marshal's uniform with plumed hat. He wore the jewel and ribbon of the Thistle. Most of his entourage wore scarlet. After the ceremony, which lasted about four hours, the King departed from Waverley for the Highlands.

When visiting Edinburgh
take Tea at RENTONS
(opposite Waverley Station)

ABOVE: TEA ROOM AT RENTONS circa 1907

Rentons was founded in 1805 at 9 North Bridge. In 1840 the firm transferred to 14 Princes Street and later took over 12 and 13 Princes Street. In 1908 Rentons purchased the building formerly occupied by Cranston and Elliot at 35-37 Princes Street. In 1927 they extended into 38-42 Princes Street. On 12 December 1935 the store was bought by C. and A. Modes Ltd., a multiple London firm of costumiers and milliners. At this time they already had branches in London, Northern England and Glasgow.

TOP RIGHT: PRINCES STREET circa 1935

Princes Street took its name after the Prince Regent. In 1769 the first houses were constructed in Princes Street at the east end. In its early stages of development Princes Street consisted of dwelling houses occupied by the nobility. However, in time, hotels, banks and warehouses began to establish themselves. The first shops were milliners and jewellers. They appeared between 1830 and 1850. When motion pictures became popular, Princes Street housed four cinemas: the Picture House (1910); the Princes Cinema (1912); the New Picture House (1913) and the Palace (1913).

BOTTOM RIGHT: N.B.R. EXPRESS LEAVING WAVERLEY circa 1906

In 1888 the 10.00 a.m. trains leaving Euston and King's Cross began to race to Edinburgh competing for passengers and prestige. Princes Street Station was the goal for the west coast companies (London North Western Railway and Caledonian Railway). Waverley Station was the finishing point for the east coast companies (Great Northern Railway and North Eastern Railway). The latter, having a slightly shorter route, completed the journey in a record seven hours 27 minutes on 7 September 1888.

Princes Street, Edinburgh.

EDINBURGH *from the Calton Hill*

ABOVE: VIEW FROM CALTON HILL *1905*

The monument on the right was built to commemorate Professor Dugald Stewart, philosopher and metaphysician. It stands close to a monument to Playfair, the astronomer. Both structures were designed by William Playfair. Dugald Stewart is buried in Canongate Churchyard.

TOP RIGHT: PRINCES STREET *circa 1903*

The picture was painted by artist David Small (1846-1927). He worked as an amateur photographer and illustrator in Dundee. The postcard shown here is part of a set of six 'Oilette' postcards published by Raphael Tuck and Sons Ltd. of London. The artist also supplied paintings of Dundee, Fife, Glasgow and the Clyde Coast, which they published as postcards.

BOTTOM RIGHT: PRINCES STREET, WEST END *1934*

The picture shows electric trams running along the centre of Princes Street. The first electric tram in Edinburgh started on 8 June 1910 and was operated by the Edinburgh and District Tramway Company. It ran between Ardmillan and Slateford to serve Gorgie markets. It was established because the power station at Tollcross could not generate sufficient power to drive a cable for cable cars at that distance. On 16 November 1956 Edinburgh's last electric tram ran from Braids to Shrubhill Depot.

Princes Street. Edinburgh.   D Small

PRINCES STREET. WEST. EDINBURGH

Jeanie Deans Cottage, Edinburgh.

RELIABLE SERIES. R1933

ABOVE: *JEANIE DEANS'S COTTAGE, ST LEONARD'S BANK circa 1904*
The cottage has been demolished, but the buildings in the background are recognisable today. The cottage overlooked the King's Park and Salisbury Crags. It has been identified as Jeanie Deans's cottage in Sir Walter Scott's *The Heart of Midlothian*. A plaque in the wall of a tenement in St Leonard's Lane marks the site of 'Jeanie Deans's Tryst' (Inn).

TOP RIGHT: *BRUNTSFIELD PLACE circa 1905*
The lands of Bruntsfield have been held for six centuries by three families, the Lauders (1381-1603), the Fairlies (1603-1695) and the Warrenders (since 1695). When Sir George Warrender succeeded to the estate in 1867, he developed the site for housing. He named the streets after members of his family — Marchmont after his wife, who was Hume Campbell, of Marchmont; Lauderdale and Thirlestane after his mother; and Spottiswoode, after his aunt, Miss Alicia Spottiswoode.

BOTTOM RIGHT: *COMISTON ROAD circa 1905*
Around 1676 Edinburgh obtained its first pure water supply which was brought from Comiston to a cistern at Castlehill. From this storage tank it was distributed in lead pipes, later replaced by elm-wood pipes, to smaller tanks or wells around the city. Water could then be collected in casks and carried to the houses. A number of these wells still remain — near John Knox's House in the High Street and at the foot of West Bow in the Grassmarket. Comiston water supply was discontinued in 1946.

Bruntsfield Place

Comiston Road

The Pier, Portobello.

New Lane, Newhaven.

ABOVE: CABLE CAR, COMELY BANK ROAD circa 1909
The Edinburgh Northern Tramway Company opened a route from Frederick Street to Comely
Bank on 17 February 1890. From July 1897 the route was operated by Edinburgh and District
Tramway Company on a 21-year lease. The poster in the window behind the driver advertises
Leith Electric Tramways' 'Grand Circular Drive'. This refers to the Granton Circle which
opened on 3 August 1909. The last Edinburgh cable car ran from the General Post Office to
Portobello on 23 June 1923.

TOP LEFT: PIER, PORTOBELLO circa 1903
The picture shows the entrance to the pier with the restaurant and concert pavilion at the far
end. The pier was designed by Thomas Bouch (1822-1880) who was responsible for the design
of the ill-fated Tay Bridge which collapsed during a storm on the night of 28 December 1879.
The pier opened in 1871 and survived until it was severely damaged by a storm in 1917 when
it was dismantled.

BOTTOM LEFT: NEWHAVEN FISHWIVES circa 1904
The Newhaven fishwives tended to inter-marry within their own communities. They are
believed to have descended from a Dutch or Fresian ancestry. Their traditional costumes
comprise a cap of cotton or linen usually covered by a shawl tied below the chin, and striped
skirts, part of which are gathered over the hips in a characteristic style. A broad belt is worn
across the forehead to support the weight of a creel or basket.

ABOVE: COLINTON VILLAGE circa 1904

The village settlement grew up around the Water of Leith where water was used to power mill machinery. Spylaw House was built for James Gillespie in 1773 beside his snuff mill. James managed the snuff factory whilst his brother John looked after their snuff shop in the High Street. The fortune left on James's death was used to found a hospital for the elderly and a free school for poor boys.

TOP RIGHT: COLINTON STATION circa 1904

Colinton Station was on a spur line from Slateford to Balerno. The line closed to passengers on 30 October 1943. Cyclists, horse-riders and walkers have used the route since. The old station platform has been repointed, walls have been rebuilt and the area landscaped. Original grinding wheels from Colinton Mill have been displayed under the arches of the viaduct. This Colinton Project work was completed in October 1981.

BOTTOM RIGHT: FEVER HOSPITAL, COLINTON circa 1903

In the 17th century plague victims and patients with infectious diseases, such as scarlet fever and diphtheria, were isolated from the population by being placed in huts near Arthur's Seat. In 1894 a temporary wooden hospital was constructed in Queen's Park during a smallpox scare. Edinburgh's Fever Hospital, today's City Hospital, was built on land bought from Colinton Mains Farm. It was opened by King Edward VII and Queen Alexandra on 13 May 1903.

olinton Station. *The address is 2ᵈ Northumberland Stre*

The Fever Hospital.   Colinton.

MURRAYFIELD BRIDGE circa 1905

ST JOHN'S ROAD, CORSTORPHINE circa 1903

BLACKHALL.

BARNTON GATE, DAVIDSON'S MAINS.

BLACKHALL *circa 1903*

BARNTON GATE, DAVIDSON'S MAINS *circa 1903*

69

Barnton Station and Burgess Golf Club House, Cramond　　　Valentines Seri

ABOVE: BARNTON STATION AND BURGESS GOLF CLUB HOUSE, CRAMOND
circa 1903

The suburban railway outer circle line was opened by the Caledonian Railway Company in 1884. The line ran from Princes Street, Dalry, Murrayfield, Craigleith (with an extension to Barnton in 1891), East Pilton (with a branch to Granton), Newhaven and Leith. The last passenger train left Barnton for Princes Street on 5 May 1951.

TOP RIGHT: OLD CRAMOND BRIG' circa 1904

The original bridge dates back to the 15th century. King James V was attacked here by a group of gypsies. He was rescued by a local miller, Jock Howieson, who brought water to bathe his wounds. The grateful King later gifted the land of Braehead to the Howiesons. In the 18th century there were corn mills and iron works between the Old Brig' and the sea which made use of water power from the river.

BOTTOM RIGHT: H.M.S. DREADNOUGHT AND FORTH BRIDGE circa 1909

Admiral Sir John Fisher (1841-1920), as First Sea Lord, was instrumental in introducing fast, powerful, well-armed and protected warships. The 1906 *Dreadnought* was the prototype. She was the fastest battleship at that time (21 knots) and the first large warship to be equipped with turbine engines. In 1909 Rosyth, on the north shore of the Firth of Forth, became a naval base. One of the first air raids of the Second World War was made on the Forth Bridge on 16 October 1939.

At Auld Cramond Brig

H.M.S. Dreadnought and Forth Bridge

Granton

ABOVE: GRANTON circa 1903

The North British Railway Company acquired the Edinburgh-Leith-Granton railway in 1847. They extended the line to Dundee by installing train ferries at Granton and Tayport. The *Leviathan*, which crossed to Burntisland, became the world's first rail ferry. A later paddle steamer, the *William Muir*, made the crossing for nearly 60 years. Granton ferry service lasted until 1940. Granton was then turned into a mine sweeping base.

TOP RIGHT: GRANTON HARBOUR circa 1910

This seaport is the creation of the Duke of Buccleuch who began developing the harbour in 1835. The development consisted of a central low-water pier 1,700 feet long and an east and west breakwater nearly double that length to shelter the pier and harbour. The development resulted in one of the best deep-water harbours on the east coast which is accessible at any state of the tide.

BOTTOM RIGHT: COALING, GRANTON HARBOUR circa 1914

Edinburgh was a coal-exporting city. Coal from Dalkeith, Tranent and some of the Fife mines was exported from Leith and Granton. Granton has been described as Edinburgh's second harbour. In 1938 a new jetty was built and equipped with a coal-loading plant.

Waverley Series 376   GRANTON HARBOUR   Smith, Goldenacre

S-763   COALING, GRANTON HARBO

ABOVE: MAIN STREET, NEWHAVEN circa 1905

Newhaven is a fishing village to the west of the Port of Leith. In 1506 James IV built a shipyard and dock here. In 1511 the *Great Michael*, the largest ship that had ever been constructed, was built for £30,000, which was an enormous sum. Since this time the port has declined in importance, but is still associated with the landing of herring.

TOP RIGHT: CHAIN PIER, TRINITY circa 1890

By 1820 steamships were becoming more popular. The shallow waters between Leith and Granton meant that passengers had to embark and disembark using rowing boats. George Crichton R.N. of the Edinburgh Steam Navigation Company, established the Trinity Pier Company. Sir Samual Brown R.N. designed and constructed the pier which opened on 14 August 1821. The pier itself fell into disuse when the harbours nearby improved. In the 1850s it became deserted and ruinous but was used by swimmers. On 17 October 1898 the pier collapsed in a storm.

BOTTOM RIGHT: OLD CHAIN PIER HOUSE, TRINITY circa 1904

The picture shows a horse bus at Chain Pier House. The service ran until 11 May 1909 when Leith Electric trams took over. The Scottish Motor Traction Company was formed on 13 June 1905. The first motorised bus service in Edinburgh began from the Mound to Corstorphine on 1 January 1906. This postcard was published by W. and A. K. Johnston Ltd., at their Edina Works in Easter Road, Edinburgh.

The Chain Pier, Trinity, Edinburgh
destroyed by Storm, Oct. 17, 1898

The Old Chain Pier House, Trinity

Carlyle's House, Comely Bank, Edinburgh.

ABOVE: *THOMAS CARLYLE'S HOUSE, 21 COMELY BANK circa 1907*
Thomas Carlyle (1795-1881), the religious and political writer, was resident at 21 Comely
Bank (1826-28) after his marriage. Thomas met his wife, Jane Welsh Carlyle (1801-1866) in 1821
and the marriage that followed was stormy, a fact that Thomas did not appreciate until after his
wife died. In 1834 the Carlyles moved to London and resided in Cheyne Row, Chelsea. It was here
that Carlyle became recognised as a writer.

TOP RIGHT: *COMELY BANK AVENUE circa 1903*
In early times the village of Stockbridge could be reached by crossing the Water of Leith via a
wooden footbridge. However, horses and carts were required to use the ford which had steep
banks on either side and also to pay a toll. Around 1786 a stone bridge was constructed. This
was replaced by a wider more level bridge in 1830.

BOTTOM RIGHT: *RAEBURN PLACE circa 1903*
Sir Henry Raeburn, Scotland's best known 18th-century painter, was born in the village of
Stockbridge on 4 March 1756. His father was a local mill owner. At the age of 16 Henry
became an apprentice to a goldsmith, James Gilliand, in Parliament Close. In his spare time
he was allowed to paint miniatures, which were in great demand. He set up a studio in George
Street in 1787 and moved to 32 York Place in 1795. He was knighted at Hopetoun House in
1822. He died after a short illness on 8 July 1823.

Comely Bank Avenue. EDINBURGH.

J. & M. S. Edin.

Raeburn Place.

J. M. Edinburgh.

Edinburgh.

50936   INVERLEITH ROW, EDINBURGH   VALENTINES SERIE

ABOVE: INVERLEITH ROW 1905

The picture shows a cable car travelling into town. The east gate to the Botanic Garden is situated on Inverleith Row. The Botanic Garden dates back to 1670 when Dr Robert Sibbald, the first Professor of Medicine at Edinburgh University, and Dr Andrew Balfour began to grow medicinal plants in a small garden near Holyrood Palace. In 1761 the garden site moved to a plot now occupied by Haddington Place. From 1820 onwards the entire collection was moved to the present site at Inverleith.

TOP RIGHT: PALM HOUSES, BOTANIC GARDEN circa 1904

The smaller of the two interconnected glasshouses, the Tropical Palm House, was opened in 1834 at a cost of £1,500. In 1858 the larger, Temperate Palm House, opened at a cost of £6,500. This glasshouse housed Britain's tallest palm tree, the cabbage palm (Livistona australis) believed to have been planted in the 1870s. By the 1980s the palm was 70 feet high and in danger of breaking through the glass. In January 1987 the tree was carefully cut. This event had been anticipated since another palm was planted in 1960.

BOTTOM RIGHT: GOLDENACRE circa 1905

On 28 January 1888 Edinburgh Northern Tramway Company's first cable car ran from Hanover Street to Goldenacre. A powerful steam engine, based at Henderson Row car shed, was used to drive the cable for this route. When the Frederick Street to Comely Bank route opened in February 1890, it was powered from the same site. Passengers for Granton were later able to change to an electric tram at Goldenacre. The first cable car service in the world started in San Francisco in 1873. London adopted the system in 1884.

Botanic Gardens, Edinburgh (Palm Houses)

GOLDENACRE

COPYRIG

R. McKAY. STATIONER

Edinburgh — Elm Row & Haddington Place

The Wrench Series No. 9009

Just a little view of our Street.

ABOVE: ELM ROW AND HADDINGTON PLACE *circa 1903*

From about 1894 to 1922, travel by tramcar between Leith and Edinburgh was awkward because the two burghs' tram systems met at the corner of Pilrig Street and Leith Walk. In 1894 each Leith tram was drawn by two horses, whilst each Edinburgh tram used four horses. In view of the gradient at the top of Leith Street, it was agreed that the tram vehicles could make the through journey, but the horses and crews had to be changed at Pilrig.

TOP RIGHT: PILRIG *1902*

As horse-drawn trams were to be faded out, Edinburgh opted for a cable car system whilst Leith decided to construct an electric tramway. This proved to be awkward for passengers who travelled between Edinburgh and Leith. The cable cars stopped at Pilrig and passengers had to transfer to a Leith tram, which was horse drawn initially. Leith introduced electric trams in 1905. In November 1920 Edinburgh and Leith amalgamated, but it was not until 20 June 1922 that an electric tram travelled from Leith to Liberton without delays at Pilrig.

BOTTOM RIGHT: FOOT OF LEITH WALK *circa 1903*

The picture shows Leith Central Station which was opened by the North British Railway Company on 1 July 1903. Certain main line trains to Glasgow or Dundee started or finished at this station. Leith Central closed on 7 April 1952 and was converted to a diesel depot. The Leith horse-drawn tramcar is shown en route to Pilrig. Many rail passengers to Edinburgh switched to travelling by tram when a through electric tram route started in 1922.

The Shore, Leith

ABOVE: SHORE, LEITH *circa 1905*
The Shore, stretching along the east bank of the Water of Leith, has recently been restored. It
is reminiscent of some of the older seaports of France. The port of Leith is one of the oldest
seaports in Britain. At the turn of the century Leith exported mainly coal, iron, spirits, ale and
paper; and imported grain, timber, chemicals and wine. There were regular passenger sailings
from Leith Harbour to London, Hull, Newcastle and to most parts of North-East Scotland.
King George IV stepped ashore at Leith on 15 August 1822 at the beginning of his state visit.

TOP RIGHT: HARBOUR, LEITH *1902*
The Harbour of Leith was given to the City of Edinburgh by Royal Charter in 1329. With
increasing trade it became necessary to make harbour improvements. In 1838 the ownership
and control of the harbour transferred to the Leith Dock Commission. Major improvements
included the building of several new docks: the Victoria (1852); Albert (1869); Edinburgh
(1881); and Imperial (1904).

BOTTOM RIGHT: JAMES PLACE FROM LEITH LINKS *circa 1910*
Leith Links is the historical home of the Honourable Company of Edinburgh Golfers. The
game was played over a five-hole course with each hole being over 400 yards long. In 1744
the first official rules were drawn up for a tournament on Leith Links and these rules, 13 in
all, formed the basis of the modern game of golf. The Links course closed in 1904 as it had
become a hazard to pedestrians.

The Sailors' Home and Tower, Leith.

LEITH FROM FERRY ROAD circa 1907

SAILORS' HOME AND TOWER circa 1904

At the Foot of Leith Walk: Corner of Great Junction Street and Kirkgate.

BERNARD STREET, LEITH.

Valentines Series

CORNER OF GREAT JUNCTION STREET AND KIRKGATE *circa* 1905

BERNARD STREET *1902*

85

ABOVE: MARLBOROUGH MANSIONS, PORTOBELLO *circa 1904*
Marlborough Mansions were built in the mid-1890s. They had elaborate wrought-iron balconies and looked more like a hotel than a traditional Scottish tenement. They were demolished in the 1960s. In front of this can be seen the entrance to the pier with the ticket office on top. The children sitting on the sand and in the rowing boats seem reluctant to expose their skin to the sun.

TOP RIGHT: SANDS, PORTOBELLO *circa 1904*
Portobello is three miles from Edinburgh on the southern shore of the Firth of Forth. During the late 19th century it developed as a holiday resort. For many Edinburgh people this was the extent of their travel out of the city. Its name was given by its founder, who built a house here in 1742 and called it Portobello, in memory of his share of Admiral Vernon's successful attack on Portobello, a seaport of Colombia. The picture is taken from the pier looking along the sands towards Joppa.

BOTTOM RIGHT: EDINBURGH CABLE AND MUSSELBURGH ELECTRIC CARS
AT JOPPA *1905*
Joppa was once a distinct village. It is now completely absorbed by Portobello. The picture is interesting since it shows the place, in Seaview Terrace, where two transport systems met. The cable car on the left is from Edinburgh. The electric tram on the right belongs to Musselburgh and District Tramway Company. After electrification of the Edinburgh system in 1923, tramcars could travel from the General Post Office to Port Seton.

The Sands, Portobello.

RELIABLE SERIES. 1529

Edinburgh Cable and Musselburgh Electric Cars at Joppa.

The Wee School, Morningside *We think your Photo very good*

ABOVE: WEE SCHOOL, MORNINGSIDE circa 1890

Morningside's village school opened in 1823. The two adults are likely to be the schoolmaster and his assistant, since there were two small classrooms inside. The picture shows 11 girls and five boys with quite a wide pupil age range. The catchment area for the school was beyond Morningside itself. Children were brought in from Swanston. When South Morningside School in Comiston Road opened in 1892, the Wee School closed.

TOP RIGHT: PRESTON STREET SCHOOL circa 1903

In June 1896 Edinburgh School Board decided that the population of the south side had increased to a point where a new school was needed. The land chosen had been the site of gallows from 1586-1761. The new school opened in September 1897. James Shearer was appointed headmaster with a salary of £340 per annum. The children were taught religious knowledge, reading, spelling, writing on slates, arithmetic, singing and gymnastics. On the outbreak of war in 1914 the school was occupied by the military. It did not return to the School Board until September 1918.

BOTTOM RIGHT: DR BELL'S SCHOOL, GREAT JUNCTION STREET, LEITH circa 1903

Andrew Bell (1753-1832), a barber's son, studied mathematics at St Andrews University before emigrating to America in 1774. After seven years working as a tutor to a Virginia plantation owner, he returned to Scotland with £800 savings and became a minister in Leith. In 1787 he sailed to India as a chaplain with the East India Company. In 1789 he became Superintendent of Madras Orphanage. Finding it impossible to obtain skilled teachers, he arranged for older children to teach younger ones. In 1797, due to ill health, he returned to Britain, where he organised schools on the Madras system. On his death he left £120,000. About half was used to found Madras College, St Andrews. The Leith school was built in 1838 and reconstructed by Leith School Board in 1892.

Preston Street School, Edinburgh.

Junction Road School   Leith.

SOUTH MORNINGSIDE PUBLIC SCHOOL, EDINBURGH   Photo. by Wohlgemuth Glasgow

BROUGHTON HIGHER GRADE SCHOOL

SOUTH MORNINGSIDE PUBLIC SCHOOL circa 1905

BROUGHTON HIGHER GRADE SCHOOL circa 1907

DAVIE STREET SCHOOL *circa 1905*

COOPER STREET SCHOOL *circa 1903*

HERIOT'S HOSPITAL, EDINBURGH.

ABOVE: HERIOT'S HOSPITAL circa 1905

George Heriot (1563-1623) was an Edinburgh jeweller to King James VI and I. On his death he left the bulk of his fortune for the education and upbringing of orphans within the city. The hospital opened with 120 boys in 1659. In 1886 Heriot's became a day school educating boys from the age of seven up to university entrance. In the same year the Governors, unable to obtain technical training for their boys, founded Heriot-Watt College. The Watt Institute and School of Art had been founded in the early 1820s as a memorial to engineer James Watt (1736-1819).

TOP RIGHT: ROYAL HIGH SCHOOL, REGENT ROAD circa 1903

The Royal High School can be traced back to a seminary attached to the Abbey of Holyrood in the 12th century. The old Burgh School of Edinburgh moved from High School Yards, off the Cowgate, to this building in 1829. King Edward VII attended the High School in 1858. The old building became the surgical department of the Royal Infirmary. Today the old building is occupied by the Geography Department of the University of Edinburgh.

BOTTOM RIGHT: ROYAL HIGH SCHOOL, INTERIOR circa 1903

Famous pupils include Sir Walter Scott (1771-1832); James Boswell (1740-1795), barrister and author; Alexander Graham Bell (1847-1922), inventor of the telephone; James Naysmith (1808-1890), the inventor of the steam-hammer; and many Lord Provosts of Edinburgh. In 1968 the school moved to Barnton. Plans were made to turn the old school into a civic art gallery and conference centre. In the end it was chosen as the site for a future Scottish Parliament.

JOHN WATSON'S INSTITUTION, DEAN, EDINBURGH.

ABOVE: JOHN WATSON'S SCHOOL, BELFORD ROAD circa 1905
John Watson, a Writer to the Signet in Edinburgh, left funds for the establishment of a school for boys and girls on his death in 1762. By 1822 the W.S. Society, who were trustees, had a sum which had accumulated to £110,000. Architect William Burn designed the school which opened in 1828. The school closed in December 1975. One hundred and fifty boys and girls tranferred to George Watson's College. The building re-opened as the Scottish Gallery of Modern Art on 14 August 1984.

TOP RIGHT: GEORGE WATSON'S COLLEGE, ARCHIBALD PLACE circa 1904
George Watson was born around 1650. He became the first accountant of the Bank of Scotland, founded in 1695. George Watson never married and on his death, on 3 April 1723, he left £144,000 for the establishment of a hospital for Edinburgh boys. The hospital, a three-storey building close to Heriot's Hospital, opened in 1741. In 1870 the hospital system was replaced by the day school system. A larger school was required. The Royal Infirmary bought the first building and the school transferred to the Merchant Maiden Hospital, Archibald Place, in 1871. The school removed to Colinton Road in 1932.

BOTTOM RIGHT: GEORGE WATSON'S LADIES' COLLEGE, GEORGE SQUARE
circa 1903
George Watson's Ladies' College is the most recent of the Edinburgh Merchant Company schools. It opened in George Square in 1871. On 26 August 1975 the college closed. Nine hundred girls joined 1,500 boys at George Watson's College in Colinton Road. The George Square building was transferred to the University of Edinburgh.

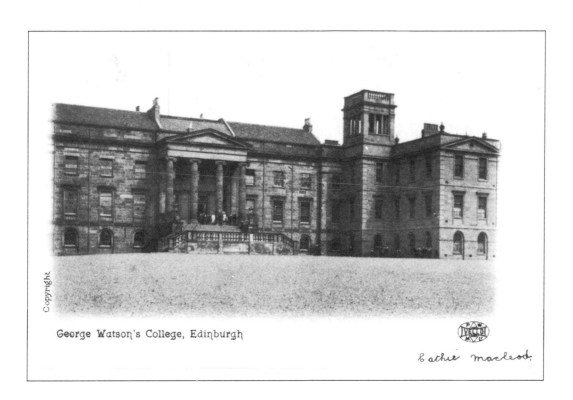

George Watson's College, Edinburgh

JAMES GILLESPIE'S OLD SCHOOL

ABOVE: JAMES GILLESPIE'S OLD SCHOOL, GILLESPIE CRESCENT circa 1910

James Gillespie was a successful tobacco and snuff merchant. He owned a snuff shop in the High Street and a snuff mill in Colinton. On his death in 1797 he left funds for the establishment of a hospital for old people and a free school for boys. The school opened in 1803 with 65 boys and was run for the next 40 years by one master. In 1870 the school moved to a new building on the same site and girls were admitted for the first time. Actor Alistair Sim was a pupil at the school. The school was demolished in 1974.

TOP RIGHT: FETTES COLLEGE circa 1904

Sir William Fettes was born on 25 June 1750. He attended the Royal High School until he was 18 when he commenced business as a wine and tea merchant in the High Street. In 1798 he became Master of the Merchant Company and in the following year he became Lord Provost. On his death on 27 May 1836 he left £166,000 for the establishment of an educational hospital. Architect David Bryce designed the college in the style of a French chateau. The college opened on 5 October 1870 under the headmastership of Dr Potts who had taught at Rugby. The trustees, going against the wishes of the founder, decided to model the school on the lines of the English public school system.

BOTTOM RIGHT: DANIEL STEWART'S COLLEGE circa 1905

Daniel Stewart, a crofter's son, was born in Logierait, Perthshire, in 1741. He moved to Edinburgh where he became an apprentice wigmaker. A client, impressed by him, invited Stewart to accompany him to India as valet. On his master's death he was left £11,000. In 1771 he obtained a post in the Court of Exchequer. On Stewart's death in 1814, never having married, he left about £20,000 for the establishment of a boys' hospital. Architect David Rhind submitted plans which had been used in a competition for the rebuilding of the Houses of Parliament, burned in 1834. This, the last of the hospitals in Edinburgh, opened with 66 pupils in 1855.

Fettes College, Edinburgh

DANIEL STEWART'S COLLEGE EDINBURGH.

97

1050. 29.　　　University and South Bridge, Edinburgh.

ABOVE: UNIVERSITY AND SOUTH BRIDGE circa 1903
In 1582 King James IV granted Edinburgh Town Council, by Royal Charter, permission to found its own college. The first students were admitted to the Kirk o' Field site in October 1583. In the 1780s the pressure of rising student numbers led to the demolition of the site. In its place, Robert Adam designed a new building — known today as Old College.

TOP RIGHT: OLD COLLEGE circa 1904
Robert Adam died in 1792. William Playfair completed the work in the 1820s using Adam's designs. The north-west corner housed the new Anatomy Theatre. William Burke and William Hare set up in partnership to supply bodies to Dr Knox. The penalties for grave robbing were severe, so many bodies were supplied before they were buried.

BOTTOM RIGHT: SURGEONS' HALL circa 1904
Surgeons' Hall was designed by William Playfair in 1832. Joseph Lister (1827-1921) held the Chair of Clinical Surgery, at Edinburgh University from 1869-77. He pioneered the use of carbolic acid and aseptic surgery.

98

Edinburgh   *University, The Old Quadrangle*

SURGEONS HALL. NICHOLSON ST. EDINBURGH.

99

University Union, Edinburgh

ABOVE: STUDENTS' UNION, TEVIOT ROW circa 1905
Teviot Row House was the world's first purpose-built Student Union. It was built with funds raised by the students themselves. It was opened by Lord Inglis, Chancellor of the University, in October 1889. The extension was added in 1906. The McEwan Lamp stands on the left with Bristo Street beyond.

TOP RIGHT: STUDENTS' UNION AND McEWAN HALL 1897
The Teviot Row Students' Union is shown on the left with the McEwan Hall to the right. Dr William McEwan M.P. donated £115,000 for the Graduation Hall which was built in 1897. Sir Walter Scott was educated at the Royal High School before entering Edinburgh University. R. L. Stevenson studied at the University in the 1870s. Sir Arthur Conan Doyle graduated from the Medical School in the 1880s. In 1893 the first women graduated from the University. The campaign to admit women to British universities had begun in 1872.

BOTTOM RIGHT: MEDICAL SCHOOL, TEVIOT PLACE 1906
The Faculty of Medicine was established in 1726. The first small infirmary was established off College Wynd in 1729. The second Royal Infirmary, designed by William Adam, was built in Infirmary Street in 1838-41. The third Royal Infirmary, designed by David Bryce, was constructed in Lauriston Place and opened in 1879. The new Medical School was the first major University development after Old College. It was completed in 1884.

M'Ewan Hall and Students' Union, Edinburgh

New University Buildings, Edinburgh

Meadow Walk, Edinburgh

ABOVE: MEADOWS *circa 1904*

The area now known as the Meadows was once a stretch of water and drinking place for elk and stag. In 1781 the horns and skull of a giant stag were dug up under the roots of an old tree in one of the sections of the Meadows. In the 16th century the city's main water supply came from the loch. In 1772 the let of the waters passed to Thomas Hope of Rankeillor. He drained the loch, built Middle Meadow Walk and also some of the side walks.

TOP RIGHT: ROYAL INFIRMARY FROM THE NORTH *circa 1903*

The picture shows the front of the Royal Infirmary, Lauriston Place, which opened in 1879. In 1903 the hospital was enlarged by the removal of buildings in Lauriston Lane. These included the Dental Hospital, George Watson's Junior School and the Royal Hospital for Sick Children, which were all re-sited. Further expansion occurred in the 1930s after the second George Watson's Boys' School was bought.

BOTTOM RIGHT: MEDICAL WARD, ROYAL INFIRMARY *1907*

Sir James Young Simpson (1811-1870), working as a gynaecologist in Edinburgh, used chloroform as an anaesthetic for the first time in place of sulphuric ether. He made the discovery on 4 November 1847 at 52 Queen Street, Edinburgh, when he inhaled chloroform and was later found collapsed under a table. Chloroform was thought to be dangerous initially. Acceptance came after Queen Victoria permitted its use in the birth of Prince Leopold in 1853.

EDINBURGH ROYAL INFIRMARY. FROM THE NORTH

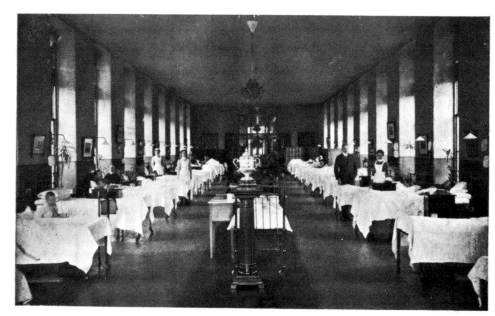

A MEDICAL WARD IN THE ROYAL INFIRMARY, EDINBURGH

ABOVE TOP RIGHT: ROYAL SCOTTISH MUSEUM circa 1903
The Royal Scottish Museum dates from 1854 when the museum was established as the Industrial Museum of Scotland. Initially old buildings on the present site formed a temporary museum. The foundation stone of the new building was laid by the Prince Consort on 23 October 1861. Exhibits on the ground floor of the main hall include architecture, sculpture, Indian arts and coins.

On 1 December 1864 the name changed to the Edinburgh Museum of Science and Art. The first section was formally opened by H.R.H. Prince Alfred, Duke of Edinburgh, on 19 May 1866. The second portion of the building was opened in January 1875 and the west wing completed in 1888. In October 1904 the name was changed to the Royal Scottish Museum.

BOTTOM RIGHT: CARNEGIE FREE LIBRARY circa 1904
The foundation stone for the Central Library was laid by Dr Andrew Carnegie (1835-1919) on 9 July 1887. Carnegie was born in great poverty in Dunfermline and emigrated to America where he developed a huge steel 'empire'. With his profits, he endowed various foundations for educational work. He provided £50,000 for this library, which was a vast sum. The building faces George IV Bridge, and has its lower storeys in the Cowgate.

Museum of Science and Art   Edinburgh

Edinburgh
Free Public Library

Waverley Series

JENNER'S, EDINBURGH.
THE MOST FASHIONABLE
SHOPPING CENTRE IN SCOTLAND

ABOVE: JENNERS circa 1905

In 1838 Charles Jenner and Charles Kennington, two draper's assistants in Leith Street, were dismissed by their employers for attending Musselburgh races. As a consequence, they decided to set up their own drapery business as 'Kennington and Jenner' and opened on 1 May 1838. They leased two shops at 47 Princes Street, on the site which they occupy today. By 1860 'Kennington and Jenner' had expanded into 48 Princes Street and occupied 2, 4, 6 and 8 South St David Street. In 1863, after the death of Charles Kennington, the store became Charles Jenner and Company. By 1875 the shop had expanded upwards on the South St David Street side. In November 1892 Jenners, then the largest retail shop in Scotland, was entirely destroyed by fire with a loss of £250,000. The new building, designed by W. H. Beattie, opened on 6 May 1895. In 1903 the old Edinburgh Stock Exchange was bought and rebuilt as part of Jenners, which enabled the store to expand up to Rose Street. In 1922 the frontage extended to 52 Princes Street.

TOP RIGHT: JOHN WIGHT AND COMPANY, 104-106 PRINCES STREET circa 1906

BOTTOM RIGHT: LOTHIAN ROAD circa 1903

SCOTLAND'S PRINCIPAL TARTAN WAREHOUSE.

JOHN WIGHT & CO.'S, 104, 105, and 106 Princes Street, Edinburgh.

Illustrated Catalogues of Golf Capes, Rugs, and Tartan Goods, POST FREE.

The Lothian Road, Edinburgh.

Phone 4767

STEWART LAMB'S
56 NORTH BRIDGE, EDINBURGH

ABOVE: STEWART LAMB'S, 56 NORTH BRIDGE circa 1915
Many firms, particularly drapers as is the case with this card, produced postcards as a means of advertising their stores. This card, sent to Miss Lawson of Gorebridge, is particularly interesting. It reads: 'Just to let you know that our sale begins on 14 January. You will see a list of bargains in Wednesday's *News* and *Dispatch*. Shall be glad to see you here soon'. The card is signed by Stewart Lamb.

TOP RIGHT: PATRICK THOMSON'S DEPARTMENT STORE circa 1911
In 1845 Patrick Thomson's father, Thomas Thomson, set up business as a linen draper at 2 Shandwick Place, Edinburgh. Three years later the firm moved to 135 Princes Street. Patrick entered the store around 1886. In 1902 the firm moved to South Bridge. In 1906 they took over the shop at 15 North Bridge and by 1910 the firm had expanded into 11, 13, 15, 17 and 19 North Bridge.

BOTTOM RIGHT: GEORGE KEDDIE, WINE MERCHANT, 39 BROUGHTON STREET
circa 1916

THEATRE ROYAL AND ST MARY'S CATHEDRAL

ABOVE: THEATRE ROYAL AND ST MARY'S CATHEDRAL circa 1923
The Broughton Street site was associated with entertainment for over 150 years. In 1790 a circus was built by Mr Jones and Mr Parker. In time the building was altered and known successively as Cotti's Concert Rooms, the Pantheon, and the Caledonian Theatre. The latter was renamed the Adelphi and destroyed by fire in 1853. The Theatre Royal which had opened in 1769 in Shakespeare Square, where the G.P.O. is today, closed in 1859. The Queen's Theatre and Opera House was built on the site of the Adelphi. The name changed to Theatre Royal in 1859. The Theatre finally closed in March 1946 after a fire.

TOP RIGHT: TARVIT STREET AND LEVEN STREET circa 1903
The picture shows Leven Lodge, originally named Drumdryan House, which occupied the site of the present-day King's Theatre. The mansion was built around 1730 by solicitor Patrick McDowall. His son built a three-storey extension and sold the house to the Earl of Leven in 1749. He used it as a country residence for several years. The tall chimney of Drumdryan brewery, established in 1760, can be seen behind the house.

BOTTOM RIGHT: KING'S THEATRE 1906
Leven Lodge finally housed a fruit shop, grocer, china shop and a corn merchant. It was demolished along with the brewery in 1905. On this site, Edinburgh Construction Company built the King's Theatre which opened on 8 December 1906 with *Cinderella*. The King's Theatre tended to specialise in pantomime and musicals. The Royal Lyceum Theatre in Grindlay Street, which opened on 11 September 1883, concentrated on drama.

A Fruit and Grain " Corner " Tarvit Street and Leven Street, Edinburgh

ABOVE: *USHER HALL circa 1914*

Andrew Usher (1826-1898), brewer and businessman, donated £100,000 in June 1896 to the city to build a public hall. The selection of a suitable site led to a long delay in its construction. The foundation stone was laid by Their Majesties King George V and Queen Mary on 19 July 1911. The Usher Hall was formally opened by Mrs Usher on 6 March 1914.

TOP RIGHT: *CRAIGLOCKHART HYDROPATHIC, SLATEFORD 1903*

Craiglockhart Hydropathic was completed in 1880, but was found to be unprofitable until it was taken over in 1890 by the Dunblane Hydropathic Company Ltd. Between 1917 and 1919 it was used as a military hospital for soldiers suffering from shell-shock. Wilfred Owen and Siegfried Sassoon were patients in 1917. Owen wrote his best poems here. He was discharged in October 1917 after a four-month stay. He returned to the front line in August 1918 and was killed in action on 4 November 1918, one week before Armistice Day. Sassoon lived until 1967.

BOTTOM RIGHT: *DONALDSON'S HOSPITAL circa 1905*

Donaldson's Hospital was designed by William Playfair in the Tudor style and completed in 1851. Its founder was James Donaldson, a West Bow bookseller, and one of the pioneers of cheap literature. He left money for the establishment of a charitable and educational institution for poor children, some of whom were deaf and dumb. In 1938 the school amalgamated with the Royal Institution for the Education of Deaf and Dumb Children in Henderson Row (founded in 1810).

The Sick Children's Hospital, Edinburgh.

ABOVE: SICK CHILDREN'S HOSPITAL circa 1903
The Royal Edinburgh Hospital for Sick Children first opened at 7 Lauriston Lane with 12 beds on 15 February 1860. On 18 May 1863 the hospital moved to Meadowside House at the foot of Lauriston Lane, which had space for 72 patients. On 2 December 1890 the hospital moved to Plewlands House, Morningside, after an outbreak of typhoid amongst the staff, which led to the demolition of Meadowside House. The new hospital in Sciennes Road was opened by H.R.H. Princess Beatrice on 31 October 1895. Initially the hospital housed 120 patients.

TOP RIGHT: BRUNTSFIELD HOSPITAL circa 1920
Dr Elsie Inglis (1864-1917) graduated in medicine, after Edinburgh University opened its medical degrees to women, in 1892 She practised medicine in Edinburgh and in 1899 she opened a nursing home for working women in George Square. In 1903 she acquired a house in the High Street which became the 'Hospice'. In 1910 the 'Hospice' amalgamated with Bruntsfield Hospital and specialised in maternity and infant care. In 1914 the War Office refused to let Dr Inglis and other women serve at the war front. The Edinburgh Suffrage Committee decided to raise funds for a hospital and by October 'Scottish Women's Hospitals' had been set up in France, Belgium, Serbia, Corsica and Russia. Elsie Inglis died on 26 November 1917 due to years of over-work. She was commemorated in the Elsie Inglis Memorial Maternity Hospital, Abbeyhill, which opened in 1925 and closed in October 1988.

BOTTOM RIGHT: CRAIGLEITH MILITARY HOSPITAL 1914
From November 1868 to 1914 the old building at the Western General Hospital was known as Craigleith Poorhouse. At the outbreak of war it was taken over by 2nd Scottish Territorial Hospital and became Craigleith Military Hospital. The first military patient was admitted on 14 August 1914. During the 1920s the building was used by Edinburgh Parish Council as a Poor Law Hospital. It was transferred to Edinburgh Town Council in 1929 and became a municipal general hospital on 16 May 1930.

6 Bruntsfield Hospital, Edinburgh.

Main Gateway, 2nd Scottish General Hospital, Craigleith, Edinburgh.

ABOVE: FIRE BRIGADE, LAURISTON PLACE *circa 1904*
The Edinburgh Fire Brigade was formed on 10 October 1824. It became the first Municipal Fire
Brigade in the United Kingdom and replaced the older Insurance Company Brigades. Its first
Firemaster was 23-year-old James Braidwood, the son of a prosperous Edinburgh cabinetmaker. He
built up a highly respected fire-fighting force from which he resigned to become Superintendent of
the London Fire Engine Establishment on 1 January 1833. James Braidwood died in Southwark,
London fighting the great fire on 22 June 1861.

TOP RIGHT: FIRE BRIGADE, LAURISTON PLACE *circa 1904*
The first great fire after the formation of the Municipal Brigade was in the High Street when
several tenement blocks and the steeple of the Tron Kirk caught fire in November 1824. The
old Theatre Royal had major fires in 1853, 1865, 1875 and 1884. In November 1892 Jenners'
shop in Princes Street caught fire. In 1873 Edinburgh got its first steam-pumped horse-drawn
fire engine. In June 1900 the new Central Fire Station opened at Lauriston Place. In 1906 the
Brigade obtained its first motorised fire engine.

BOTTOM RIGHT: EDINBURGH FIREMEN, HIGH STREET *circa 1860*
The picture shows Edinburgh firemen about to perform a fire drill display wearing brigade
uniform of 1824. The uniform consisted of blue jackets with brass buttons, leather helmets,
white canvas trousers and leather belts to which were attached axes, hose couplings and
spanners. The total force was divided into four groups, each under the command of a
captain and sergeant. The groups were distinguished by the separate colours, blue, red, grey
and yellow, of their helmets.

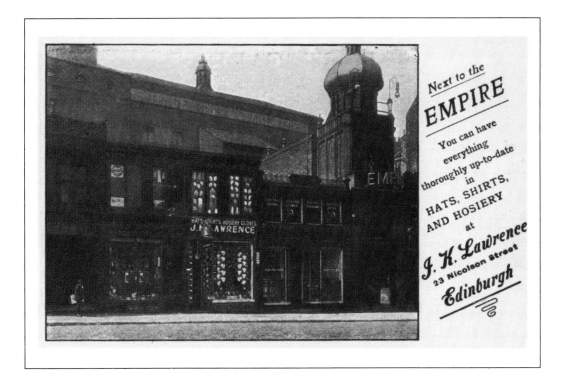

ABOVE: EMPIRE PALACE THEATRE *circa 1913*

This card was produced to advertise J. K. Lawrence's drapery store and shows its position in relation to the Empire Theatre. The Empire Palace Theatre opened on 7 November 1892. However, on 9 May 1911 there was a tragic fire which resulted in the loss of ten lives, including that of the stage performer 'The Great Lafayette'. Lafayette's real name was Sigmund Neuberger (1871-1911), a German, born of Jewish parents. He was an illusionist of international acclaim and enjoyed huge popularity.

TOP RIGHT: EMPIRE PALACE THEATRE *10 May 1911*

Lafayette was a loner whose only friend appeared to be a bull terrier called Beauty, given to him by escapologist Harry Houdini. On 1 May 1911 Lafayette's show opened at the Empire and all was well until 6 May when Beauty died of apoplexy. Lafayette had difficulty finding a burial ground for his dog. However, the Edinburgh and Portobello Cemetery Company agreed to Beauty's burial at Piershill Cemetery provided that Lafayette, on his death, would be buried with him.

BOTTOM RIGHT: FUNERAL OF 'THE GREAT LAFAYETTE', PIERSHILL CEMETERY *14 May 1911*

Lafayette tragically died in a fire which started at the end of his act on 9 May 1911. The safety curtain failed to drop fully down. It protected the audience but caused a draught which enlivened the fire on the stage. A body, believed to be Lafayette's, was sent to be cremated in accordance with Lafayette's wishes. This body was later found to be Lafayette's stage double, when the body of the real Lafayette was found by firemen beneath the stage. Lafayette's ashes were buried along with his dog at Piershill Cemetery.

EMPIRE PALACE RUINS.

Funeral of The Great Lafayette
Entering Piershill Cemetery.

ROYAL REVIEW THE GRAND STAND 18/9/05

ABOVE: GRANDSTAND, ROYAL REVIEW, HOLYROOD PARK 18 September 1905
The grandstand had space for 5,000 ticket holders who had to be in place by 10.00 a.m., one hour before the King arrived. Probably one of the best all-round views was obtained from a stand erected by William Younger & Company Ltd. above their brewery in South Back, Canongate. The weather was kind, which had not been the case when Queen Victoria reviewed the Volunteers in the pouring rain on 25 August 1881.

TOP RIGHT: SCOTS GREYS' MEMORIAL, UNVEILING CEREMONY 16 November 1906
The monument was erected to commemorate fallen heroes of the Royal Scots Greys. The trooper on horseback is wearing the regimental uniform used by the Greys when they marched out of the city in 1899 to fight in the South African War. The ceremony started at noon in the rain. Lord Rosebery unveiled the monument by removing a Union Jack which had been blowing about in the wind. Dismounted troopers in scarlet coats can be seen on the right.

BOTTOM RIGHT: LAYING THE FOUNDATION STONE,
COLLEGE OF ART 11 July 1907
A half-day holiday was declared by many shopkeepers. This swelled the crowds which had gathered early to watch the Prince and Princess of Wales drive into Lauriston from Dalkeith Palace. On arrival at the Fire Station the Lord Provost gave an address of welcome. The Prince met members of the Town Council and some of the donors of the Art School fund. After laying the foundation stone, he went on to visit the Royal Infirmary before returning to Dalkeith.

H.R.H. Prince of Wales laying the Foundation Stone, Edinburgh New Art School—July 11, 1907

The King and Queen Opening Colinton Mains Hospital, May 13, 1903.

RELIABLE [RS] SERIES.

ABOVE: KING AND QUEEN OPENING COLINTON MAINS HOSPITAL 13 May 1903
The new Fever Hospital was officially opened by King Edward VII and Queen Alexandra, shown in the picture with Lord Provost James Steel. The hospital was built on an isolated site, on the outskirts of Edinburgh, and strict isolation was maintained for the patients. Each patient was given a reference number, and daily reports were issued in local newspapers alongside these code numbers. Relatives were able to visit if requested in the newspaper.

TOP RIGHT: ROYAL VISIT 18 July 1911
This week, the Picture House in Princes Street was showing the investiture of the Prince of Wales at Carnaervon which had taken place on 12 July 1911. In addition, all the daily occurrences of the Royal Visit to Edinburgh were shown. King George V and Queen Mary arrived at the Caledonian Station on 17 July. The next day they visited St Giles Cathedral, the Castle, and the Royal Scottish Academy. On 19 July they laid the foundation stone at the Usher Hall and visited the Royal Infirmary. On 20 July new colours were presented to the 2nd Battalion Royal Scots. On the 21st they departed for London from Waverley Station.

BOTTOM RIGHT: FUNERAL OF QUINTINSHILL RAILWAY DISASTER VICTIMS
24 May 1915
On 22 May 1915 half a battalion of the 7th Royal Scots set off from Leith by train on a journey which should have taken them to Liverpool, where a ship was waiting to sail to Turkey. At Quintinshill, near Gretna Green, the troop train crashed into a stationary local train diverted on to the same line in error, to allow a sleeper train to pass in the opposite direction. The sleeper train then crashed into the wreckage. The enquiry revealed that signalmen James Tinsley and George Meakin were to blame for the 227 killed and 246 injured. Leith soldiers were buried at Rosebank Cemetery.

THE ROYAL PROGRESS TO ST. GILES-AT THE POST OFFICE.

H.M. King George 16th July 1911.

FUNERAL OF 100 VICTIMS OF THE GRETNA GREEN RAILWAY DISASTER AT LEITH
WITH MILITARY HONOURS.
The long line of transport waggons containing the coffins passing through the town to the
cemetery.

ABOVE: OPENING OF SCOTTISH NATIONAL EXHIBITION, SAUGHTON PARK
1 May 1908
The exhibition was opened by H.R.H. Prince Arthur of Connaught. The picture shows him, wearing a Scots Greys officer's uniform, in the carriage talking to Lord Provost Gibson. They had taken lunch at the North British Station Hotel before being driven through crowded streets to the Gorgie entrance, shown here. After the opening ceremony, held in the Concert Hall, the Prince toured the many exhibits. After a two-hour stay the Royal Party drove to Murrayfield polo ground to inspect a gathering of the Boys' Brigade.

TOP RIGHT: SCOTTISH NATIONAL EXHIBITION 1908
The picture shows Balgreen Road on the left with the Gorgie entrance, over the Water of Leith, on the far left in the distance. The domed building in the lower left of the picture was the Concert Hall. Its entrance faced Van Houten's exhibit, a bandstand, and the large Industrial Hall with its two towers. The Machines Hall, lower centre, faced the Fine Art Building with Saughton House beyond. Other exhibits included Winter Gardens, a native village, a model hospital, a sports ground, water chute and maze. Valentine and Sons Ltd., of Dundee, produced the official postcards and exhibition guide.

BOTTOM RIGHT: INDUSTRIAL HALL, SCOTTISH NATIONAL EXHIBITION 1908
At stand number 124 John Wight & Company of Princes Street demonstrated hand-loom tartan weaving. Stand number 209 was occupied by Peter Scott & Company Ltd., of Hawick. They had a large piece of knitting machinery producing the famous 'Pesco' underwear from 'Pesco' yarn. Operating at 96,512 stitches a minute, every garment was guaranteed unshrinkable. Robert Maule & Son of Princes Street occupied a central position in the hall with demonstrations of needlework, silk weaving and glove manufacture. Some of the buildings from the exhibition were re-erected at Marine Gardens, Portobello, which opened as an amusement park in 1910.

Scottish National Exhibition, Edinburgh, 1908

The Industrial Hall, Scottish National Exhibition.
Edinburgh, 1908

ABOVE: *ENGLAND V. SCOTLAND, RUGBY INTERNATIONAL 19 March 1904*
Rugby internationals were held at Inverleith. The card shows J. E. Crabbie (Edinburgh Academicals) throwing in from touch, marked by English left winger E. J. Vivyen (Devonport). Scotland won 6-3. The referee is shown wearing plus-fours, jacket and a cloth cap. Murrayfield rugby ground opened on 25 March 1925. In the first match Scotland beat England 14 points to 11.

TOP RIGHT: *VARDON-BRAID MATCH, MURRAYFIELD 30 July 1904*
Joiner James Braid played for Edinburgh Thistle Golf Club in his amateur days. He went on to become five times British Open Champion. The picture shows him playing Harry Vardon at Murrayfield Club in a match which attracted about 3,000 spectators. The record for the course was 70. The match ended all even with each player scoring 68. Each player completed the 14th hole, 'Sky Park', in four.

BOTTOM RIGHT: *LEITH ATHLETIC V. ALBION ROVERS 25 August 1906*
The picture shows a Scottish League Second Division match played at Logie Green, Edinburgh, before a crowd of 3,000 spectators. The visitors had a better game during the first half. They crossed over with a goal lead scored by Main, the inside-right. Halfway through the second half Walker equalised, and a minute later Wallace scored the winning goal for Leith. Leith Athletic Football Club (1887-1954) became Second Division Champions in 1939.

The Vardon-Braid Match at Murrayfield, 30th July 1904.
The 14th Hole, "Sky Park."

LEITH'S RECORD, DOUBLE CHAMPIONSHIP FLAGS. 1905—1906
LEITH V ALBION ROVERS. 25TH AUGT 1906. RESULT. 2—1 FOR LEITH

SELECT BIBLIOGRAPHY

Byatt, A., *Picture Postcards and their Publishers* (Golden Age Postcard Books, 1978)
Cameron, J. R., *The First 100 Years 1879-1979* (George Stewart and Co. Ltd., 1979)
Cant, M., *Villages of Edinburgh, Volume 1* (John Donald Publishers Ltd., 1986)
Cant, M., *Villages of Edinburgh, Volume 2* (John Donald Publishers Ltd., 1987)
Cronshaw, A., *Old Dundee Picture Postcards* (Mainstream Publishing Co. Ltd., 1988)
Durie, A. J., *George Washington Wilson in Edinburgh* (Aberdeen University Library, 1986)
Easton, D. (Editor), *By the Three Great Roads — A History of Tollcross, Fountainbridge and the West Port* (Aberdeen University Press, 1988)
Footman, R. and Young, B., *Edinburgh University — An Illustrated Memoir* (University of Edinburgh, 1983).
Guthrie, D., *The Royal Edinburgh Hospital for Sick Children 1860-1960* (E. and S. Livingstone Ltd., 1960)
Hannavy, J., *A Moment in Time — Scottish Contributions to Photography 1840-1920* (Third Eye Centre Ltd., 1983)
Hill, C. W., *Discovering Picture Postcards* (Shire Publications, 1970)
Hunter, D. L. G., *Edinburgh's Transport* (Advertiser Press, 1964)
Macgregor, F., *The Story of Greyfriars Bobby* (Ampersand, 1980)
Macgregor, F., *The Scots Magazine* (D. C. Thomson, January 1989)
McKean, C. and Walker, D., *Edinburgh — An Illustrated Architectural Guide* (R.I.A.S./Scottish Academic Press, 1982)
Minto, C. S., *Victorian and Edwardian Edinburgh from Old Photographs* (Batsford Ltd., 1973)
Minto, C. S. and Armstrong, N. E. S., *Edinburgh Past and Present* (Oxford Illustrated Press, 1975)
Murray, A., *The Forth Railway Bridge* (Mainstream Publishing Co. Ltd., 1986)
Post Office Edinburgh and Leith Directory (G.P.O., various dates)
Reid, A., *"Aye Ready!" — The History of Edinburgh Fire Brigade* (Edinburgh Fire Brigade, 1974)
Smith, C. J., *Historic South Edinburgh Volume 1* (Charles Skilton Ltd., 1978)
Smith, C. J., *Historic South Edinburgh Volume 2* (Charles Skilton Ltd., 1979)
Smout, T. C., *A Century of the Scottish People 1830-1950* (Fontana, 1986)
Ward,, J. and Stevenson, S., *Printed Light* (Scottish National Portrait Gallery, H.M.S.O., 1986)
Waugh, H. L. (Editor), *George Watson's College History and Record 1724-1970* (George Watson's College, 1970)